I'll Pray for You:

A Christian Woman's Guide to Surviving Domestic Violence

DONNA WAYLES

Published by Kharis Publishing, imprint of Kharis Media LLC.

Copyright © 2020 Donna Wayles

ISBN-13: 978-1-946277-77-0
ISBN-10: 1-946277-77-0
Library of Congress Control Number: 2020943751

Unless otherwise noted, Scriptures are taken from the King James Version of the Bible in the public domain. Scriptures noted NKJV are quoted from the New King James Version of the Bible, Copyright © 1982 by Thomas Nelson. Used by permission. All rights reserved. Scriptures quoted as NIV are taken from the New International Version of the Bible. Copyright ©1973, 1978, 1984, 2011 by Biblica, Inc. Used by permission. All rights reserved worldwide.

All Kharis Publishing products are available at special quantity discounts for bulk purchases. For details, contact:
Kharis Media LLC
Tel: 1-479-599-8657
support@kharispublishing.com
www.kharispublishing.com

A WORD FROM THE AUTHOR

Bruised, desperate and homeless, I stood on the back porch of the head deacon's house. I expected him to welcome us with open arms. After all, he had helped us before. However, when I explained my situation, something was different this time. He didn't invite us inside. Instead, he shook his head, saying, "I'm sorry. I've done all I can, but **I'll pray for you**." I couldn't believe what I was hearing. With nowhere to go, I walked to my car, defeated, and drove away.

But, when I doubted everything and my life was in shambles, God showed me that although I had nothing left, He was all I needed. My faith transformed from merely doing my duty to having a deeply personal relationship with God. Through all the heartache, He has blessed me "exceedingly abundantly above all that I could ask or think," (Ephesians 3:20 KJV).

DISCLAIMER

The events and conversations in this book are recalled to the best of the author's ability, although some names and details were changed to protect the safety and privacy of individuals. This book is not intended to castigate or put down another person. It is merely a retelling of events as the author lived and remembered them. This work is a celebration of God's faithfulness, who heals and helps us recover from the difficulties of life.

CONTENTS

PROLOGUE

"I will never leave thee, nor forsake thee." – Hebrews 13:5b KJV

How did my life get to be like this? This question haunted me as I drove the thirty minutes to the apartment on the military base that I had once shared with Dirk, my soon-to-be ex-husband. I had called the MPs, or military police, who were on duty. I was not allowed to go on base without their knowledge because of Dirk's continuing threats. They were to meet me at the apartment so I could feed and care for my cats. I knew our marriage had problems, but I never dreamed of my life being in danger. After Dirk assaulted me, the MPs had arrested him and, during the questioning, he had warned NCIS detectives, "I will finish the job if I get the chance." I was in grave danger.

When I met the MPs at my apartment, they explained there would always be three of them. This was the protocol in a domestic violence situation. The MPs took my keys and instructed me to wait outside the apartment while they checked everywhere for any evidence of Dirk's being there. The empty cans of energy drinks, potato chip bags, and candy bar wrappers revealed he had been in the apartment.

The MPs looked for traps or other devices he may have rigged to hurt me. They opened every drawer, cabinet, and closet. They even patted down the couch and chair cushions before allowing me to sit down. I could not go inside until they had totally "tossed" the house.

After being allowed inside, I quickly fed my cats, petting them to assure them I would be back for them soon--at least I hoped I would. Emotions of fear, sadness, and disappointment began to swirl around within me. But I didn't have time for those feelings now. Forcing myself to focus on my immediate needs, I grabbed

a few more baby clothes for my twenty-month-old daughter, Ally, and a couple of clean outfits for me. I left promptly. The MPs locked the apartment and escorted me to my car. They watched as I pulled away.

Staying in hiding at the home of my friend, Chloe, I struggled to maintain a sense of "normalcy" for my daughter and myself. I was having trouble sleeping and was waking in a panic, knowing Dirk was determined to hurt me. As I walked downstairs, I would freeze in fear. I forced myself to hold the handrail and assured myself that I was okay. I was not eating well and was losing weight. The doctors diagnosed me as "depressed."

Depressed? I couldn't possibly be "depressed." I had been taught the Bible in church. I was raised to believe that depression is a sin and the result of not trusting enough in God to take care of my life. But how could I conceivably trust a God who would let me be hurt so deeply? I now doubted everything I had ever heard about or read in the Bible.

1. THE BEGINNING

"Therefore, my beloved brethren, be ye steadfast, unmovable, always abounding in the work of the Lord, forasmuch as ye know that your labor is not in vain in the Lord." - I Corinthians 15:58 KJV

I went to church every Sunday for as long as I could remember. My parents made sure my younger brother and I were in church whenever the doors were open. We attended Sunday school, Sunday morning service, Sunday night service, even Wednesday night prayer meeting.

I was born into a Christian family. My great uncle and great grandfather were ministers in the isolated mountain communities of upstate New York. Continuing the family tradition, my parents, grandparents, aunts, and uncles served God in their churches and Christian summer camps.

When I was old enough to attend school, my parents, along with the other members of their Bible study life group, became the founding committee of our church's Christian school. At the Christian school, I memorized entire books of the Bible in the King James Version. I won numerous awards for Scripture memory and Christian character, in addition to my academic awards. I sang in the choir and worship team, as well as taught Sunday school and children's church. I loved being a "good girl."

I trusted God as my Heavenly Father. I had memorized His promise, "For I know the thoughts that I think toward you, saith the Lord, thoughts of peace, and not of evil, to give you an expected end," (Jeremiah 29:11 KJV). I was convinced that doing all the "dos" and not doing the "don'ts" would make God pleased with me, and He would bless me.

One couple from my parents' Bible study life group, Mary and John, had a farm that went bankrupt and, sadly, the financial stress led them to divorce. As a child, this was the first time I had ever heard of anyone getting a divorce. We were never allowed to speak of it, except to quote, "For the Lord, the God of Israel, saith that He hates putting away…therefore, take heed to your spirit, that ye deal not treacherously," (Malachi 2:16 KJV). I understood from this verse that if someone "puts away" or divorces their spouse, they are "doing violence to the one he [she] should protect," (Malachi 2:16 NIV). God considers divorce as dangerous as treason: the betrayal of someone who should protect you.

The church taught us that divorce was not allowed for any reason. God is good and promises to forgive. "If we confess our sins, He is faithful and just to forgive us our sins and to cleanse us from all unrighteousness," (I John 1:9 KJV). In God's eyes, all sin is wrong. As believers in Jesus Christ, we are responsible that "if a man [or woman] be overtaken in a fault, ye which are spiritual, restore such a one in the spirit of meekness; considering thyself, lest thou also be tempted," (Galatians 6:1 KJV) Sadly, I watched as John, Mary, and their children quietly left our church and did not return. I missed my friends, but I knew that God would bless me with a good life if I continued following the church's rules.

I spent the summers of my high school years attending Christian camp, teaching Bible clubs, and helping out at my church. I praised God as children came to faith in Jesus. I planned to attend a Christian college. I felt drawn to education, but I resisted the idea of God's leading me to become a teacher. My great Aunt Dorothy had taught in a one-room schoolhouse in the mountains of upstate New York. I knew how difficult it had been for her at times. All the Christian school teachers I knew did not make much money, and they usually switched schools every few years. They sacrificed money and stability to "do God's will." I'm not ashamed to say I was hoping to dedicate my life to a career that offered more financial security but, still, I couldn't shake the conviction that teaching was God's plan for me.

I had developed a flawless five-year plan for my college experience. I'd meet and fall in love with a good, Christian man, maybe in one of my classes or campus activities, and we'd date through college. He'd propose during our senior year, and we'd get married after graduation. We'd honeymoon somewhere warm and set up our own home just in time for me to start my stable, well-paid accounting job, where I would work until we had our first baby. We would find a community-oriented church and serve God together. Easy, right?

Have you ever heard the expression, "When we make plans, God laughs?" It turns out God had a very different plan than the one I'd dreamed up. I began college studying to be in business management or accounting. I felt a little guilty that my dream job wasn't as all-in for God like the girls who wanted to be missionaries, or social workers, and the boys who wanted to become pastors. I rationalized that I would give money to those missionaries and pastors. After all, someone has to support them.

To begin with, nothing was going according to plan on the dating front either. I joined my roommate's sorority and became one of the intermural cheerleaders for our brother fraternity. Those weekend soccer, football, and baseball games were the place to see and be seen on campus. I felt sure I'd meet the right guy for me there.

One rainy night, I was cheering on my team when a handsome guy came out of the crowd to stand next to me. He held a large golf umbrella over my head as he introduced himself. "Hi, I'm Paul. I'm in your sorority's brother fraternity." He asked if I minded him holding the umbrella, and I replied that I didn't care, but that I didn't want to risk smacking him during our cheer routine.

He asked me on a date to the snack shop the next evening, and I agreed. After talking and laughing for several hours, he asked me to meet him for lunch the following Monday. Soon we were dating. Of course, our dates were mostly lunches or group outings since I was a "good girl" who didn't want to move too fast. Honestly, I would describe our pace as glacial! But several months later, Paul got into trouble for drinking alcohol. His punishment was that he was no longer allowed to participate in any extra-curricular activities or socialize with members of the opposite sex. He was grounded. I felt very uncomfortable dating someone who would get himself into so much trouble. After talking it over with my prayer group and my close friends, I decided that Paul was not the man for me. We broke up. The night before Christmas break, Paul called my dorm room out of the blue. He flatly stated that "in a dream, God revealed that we should marry each other.

Without hesitating, I blurted out, "Shouldn't God have revealed that to me, too?" I would not marry him. "Please, don't call me ever again," I told him.

Returning to college after the semester break, Paul's sister caught me in the hallway to say, "Paul got expelled from the college. I'm glad you weren't involved."

"Thanks for telling me," I replied. I breathed a sigh of relief and said a prayer of thanks to God. I had dodged a bullet, and I knew that it was God who had made sure I saw Paul's true colors and saved me from marrying the wrong person.

I felt that I was submitting to God's calling by committing to a double major in accounting and business education. I wanted to teach in a Christian school. I worked as a student teacher in the last semester of my senior year. I spent a significant amount of time watching Ms. Hein, plan lessons during our lunch breaks, and waiting for the copier machine to make all 200 copies of student worksheets. We talked about my plans, her twenty-five-year teaching career, and advice on how I could become a better teacher. To my amazement, she could make a student stop disrupting class with only a stern look. She explained that sometimes to avoid drawing attention to the student who is not doing what they are supposed to, all I should do is stand by the student or give them the "teacher look."

One recurring conversation revolved around Ms. Hein's niece, a preschooler, diagnosed with cancer. She had become an unbeliever who felt angry with God. She could not understand how I could serve a God who would allow a child to suffer from this disease. I didn't have answers for her, or myself either, to be honest. I don't know why God allows children to hurt, or why bad things to happen to good people. But I believed, "the God of all grace, who hath called us unto his eternal glory by Christ Jesus, after that ye have suffered a while, make you perfect, stablish, strengthen, settle you," (I Peter 5:10 KJV). I shared my certainty that God is with His children, even in their suffering. I trusted Him.

God has shown us in His Word that He can be trusted. He commands, "Trust in the Lord with all your heart and lean not on your own understanding. In all thy ways acknowledge Him, and He shall direct your path," (Proverbs 3:5 KJV). God urges us to trust Him, and when we do, He is there to care for us. He repeats, "Commit thy way unto the Lord; trust also in Him, and He shall bring it to pass," (Psalm 37:5 KJV). When I decided to serve God as a teenager, He directed me to opportunities that let me do good things. My confidence in God grew as I experienced God's goodness. I understood that when I trusted Him and did good things, He was good to me. Although bad things happen, God uses these times to strengthen and teach us.

I thought I had grown through some of my struggles with student teaching. I still had trouble giving the "teacher look," but my college professor who evaluated me as I taught several lessons graded me with a "B." It wasn't the "A" I had hoped for, but I was passing. However, I was in for a surprise. Behind my back, Ms. Heins had told my professor that she was very concerned about my "poor teaching skills" and "bad classroom management." At the end of the semester, Ms. Heins wrote my recommendation as "she should not be a classroom teacher." My grade was a C-.

I was discouraged. Seeing such a negative comment made me have second thoughts. Did I want to be a teacher? Was all the hard work I had put in worth it? Would anyone hire me to be a teacher? What if I failed? Should I go into business management after all?

My decision clearly needed a lot of thought. What was the hurry? I would be working for the rest of my adult life. Before I took on all that responsibility, I wanted to spend the summer serving God as part of the Hawaii mission team. The flights, food, and lodging would be costly. Since I didn't know how we would be able to afford it, I made a deal with my parents: if God provided the money, I would be allowed to go on a mission trip.

After writing and rewriting several drafts, I finally mailed a letter explaining my mission trip and asking my friends and family for their prayers and financial support. The responses seemed to come almost daily with an encouraging message and a check for $10 or $20. Within a few weeks, I had reached my goal. God had provided the money for me to go on the mission trip!

I had trusted God to allow me to serve Him in Hawaii, and He had provided the money. As I read my morning devotions, "Seek ye first the kingdom of God and His righteousness, and all these things shall be added unto you," (Matthew 6:33 KJV), God honored my desire to serve Him and provided the opportunity. I had heard missionaries share stories of God sending them money just before the bills were due, but now I plainly saw God send the money for me! This small miracle gave me more confidence that I could trust Him to take care of me. He knew, before I did, how much this mission trip would change my life.

My group was assigned to help a pastor of a mostly-military church in Honolulu. He lived with his family in a three-bedroom apartment on a high floor of a downtown apartment building. I shared a bedroom with their two older girls. The youngest daughter, a toddler, slept in her parents' room, and the third bedroom functioned as the church office and pastor's study. I was surprised at how happy and content they were in serving God, despite having very little money, young children, and living in such a small place.

We happily did everything they asked, teaching five-day Bible clubs for children, painting, decorating bulletin boards, and visiting people to invite them to attend our church. One afternoon we pulled up old, wet, moldy carpeting because a pipe in another pastor's house burst, and he could not afford to have it professionally done. I followed all the dos and don'ts as I understood them from my church's teaching. I was the perfect product of years of training.

∞

After the mission trip, I moved back home with my parents, who were pressuring me to find a job. Excited by all the good wishes and blessings I received as part of the mission team, I knew God would lead me to the right position. I just hadn't found it yet. I had college loans and bills to pay; my parents would help, but I was an adult who needed to pay my own way. I went to several unsuccessful job interviews. I trusted God to send the right job my way, but when? "I waited patiently for the Lord, and He inclined unto me and heard my cry," (Psalms 40:1 KJV). In answer to my prayers, and I'm sure my parents' prayers as well, one August afternoon I got a call from a Christian school in South Carolina desperately needing a teacher. The school and church seemed reasonable. Required church attendance was not a problem as I was joining part of a church ministry. I had been attending church routinely, so I was not worried. I accepted their job offer.

As a first-year teacher, I planned for everything to go smoothly; however, things did not always go as planned. One morning during my sixth-grade math class, a boy yelled out to me, "Look, I have a loose tooth." I smiled and said, "Thanks for sharing, but maybe tell me before or after class?"

His fingers being still in his mouth should have been a warning to me, but no. I asked the students to grade each other's work as I read off the answers to the previous night's homework, just as we did most days. Then, hearing a loud, "Oops!" I looked up from my answer key to see his tooth come flying towards me. After a bounce and some rolling, it stopped under the whiteboard in the front of the classroom. I took a quick deep breath and hoped my voice sounded calm. "Please, get a tissue, pick up your tooth, and then go to the nurse." He quickly did as I asked.

As he closed the door behind him, the other students looked at me with faces showing their confusion, as if to say, "what just happened?" I commented, "So, let's not do that again."

Afterward, I tried to continue the lesson with very little success. I'm pretty sure the students didn't learn anything that day, but I am sure they remember the tooth.

During this time, the husband of Sarah, one of my friends and fellow teachers at the Christian school, left her for a younger woman. She now had two teenage children to raise on her own. The church and Christian school administration believed divorce was evil, so they demoted her to part-time status. I watched in horror as she lost her job with no safety net. I wanted to help, but I did not want to lose my own job. I kept my opinions to myself, following the church.

∞

At the end of the school year, I went on the Hawaii mission team again. I was thrilled at another opportunity to serve God in Hawaii. I served at the same church as the previous summer. Once again I was thrilled to be able to help pastors, teach Bible clubs, and sing in worship services at several of the churches.

At a fellowship time after one of the worship services, a Christian school principal approached me and wondered if I would be interested in teaching in Hawaii. "Yes, of course," I answered without hesitating, and then I asked, "Are you joking?"

He liked to "talk story" as the Hawaiian locals called it, but he assured me that he was not. Since I had previously signed a contract for the Christian school in South Carolina, I told him that I would not break that contract. Amazingly, he held the job for me for an entire year. I was thrilled at the prospect.

2. LIVING IN HAWAII

"Therefore, my beloved brethren, be ye steadfast, unmovable, always abounding in the work of the Lord, forasmuch as ye know that your labor is not in vain in the Lord."– I Corinthians 15:58 KJV

I was ecstatic to be moving to Hawaii—to teach at a Christian school and live in paradise. I could not wait to get back to the gorgeous views, blue water, and tropical warmth. With the school's help, I had already rented a bedroom in an apartment with a married couple.

Since I had been to Hawaii as part of the mission team, I already knew I would attend the same church I had participated in during the summer. I was expecting to jump right back in with the church family, and I was not disappointed. I taught Children's Church, participated in young adult Bible studies, and the church singles' group. Each of these activities, along with my school obligations, kept me very busy. I was delighted to be about the Lord's business.

I met many incredible military personnel and local people in Hawaii. I was encouraged by the happiness of my pastor and his family in serving God, despite their meager income. Through the sermons and Bible studies, I learned more about the Bible and was able to explain what I believed to others. I went door-to-door, inviting people to church and their children to our Bible clubs.

At the church singles' ministry, besides our regular Bible study time, we met to play sports, eat out, and spend time at the beaches. Most of the singles were men—Navy sailors and Marines. I was hoping God would lead me to meet the right Christian man to marry there at the church in Hawaii. So far, it seemed God was not putting the right man in place. I went on plenty of dates, but no one struck me as the one for me. Some of the dates were great, like the Marine Corps Birthday Ball in Waikiki, and some were less fun, like the Marine who took me out for ribs saying that "if a woman loves you, she will eat ribs in front of you." To him, eating ribs required even the most proper of women to let her guard down and dig in! It was a fun, if messy date, but we just didn't have sparks. I dated Sam, a submariner who rode a cherry red motorcycle. He was a lot of fun, but I realized early on that no one could ever love him as much as he loved himself. That was when I stopped saying yes to dates with him!

Every Sunday after the morning service, our pastor and his wife hosted a home-cooked meal for the singles. I loved helping prepare and serve the meal, as well as the friendship and fun with the guys. We laughed as we got to know each other by answering the pastor's silly questions. He had designed conversation starters that helped put people at ease. The discussions ranged from our favorite sports and where we were from—before Hawaii—to foods and which pasta noodle was our favorite. At the end of the meal, the person with the "faith plate" had the privilege of washing the dishes.

The faith plate was a regular dinner plate with the word "faith" printed in permanent marker on the bottom. This dish was a clear reminder of the verse, which says, "I will shew thee my faith by my works," (James 2:18b KJV). No one minded getting the faith plate and, honestly, almost everyone helped with the cleanup, regardless of who's turn it was. I was so grateful for the singles group. It helped me feel more at home in Hawaii and gave me an encouraging and supportive community. Not every church offers singles programs, and I felt fortunate that mine did.

∞

After a double date one evening, my friends and I were walking along Waikiki Beach late at night when we heard a couple arguing. The man looked as if he were going to beat up the woman. My friend, Rachel, and I were scared, but the Marines we were with said, "Stay here. We're going to take care of this." They broke up the argument, sending the couple on their way.

That incident was the first time I had ever witnessed domestic violence. Little did I know it would not be the last.

3. MEETING DIRK

"For I know the thoughts that I think toward you, saith the Lord, thoughts of peace, and not of evil, to give you an expected end." – Jeremiah 29:11 KJV

One of the summer events everybody looked forward to was the church picnic. We invited anyone and everyone in the local community to come and join us. The multi-cultural aspects of Hawaii were on full display at this picnic. From the local Hawaiian food to Filipino *lumpia* and American potato salad, our picnic had something for everyone.

Besides all of the fantastic food, there were activities set up for everyone to enjoy, including horseshoes, sack races, egg-on-a-spoon relay races and, of course, a water balloon toss. But my favorite activity was always the beach volleyball games. Two Marines, James, and Matt, challenged my friend Rachel, and me to a match. Rachel and I had both played on our high school volleyball teams, and we had a reputation for being difficult to beat! Despite a couple of scrapes from the rocks that should not have been in the sand court, Rachel and I won the hard-fought game.

After everyone had eaten and had time to play, a traveling minister gave a devotion. I sat between Sam and his new roommate, Dirk. Sam elbowed me, and whispered, "Share your Bible with Dirk; he needs it!" It was the first time I had ever met Dirk. He followed along in my Bible as the preacher spoke. At the invitation when the service concluded, Dirk went forward to make a profession of faith in Christ. I was touched that Dirk had come to know the Lord at our church picnic. I hoped that he would keep coming around.

Dirk's roommates convinced him to start coming to church and our singles group, so I got to know him over the next few weeks. He shared that he was from Florida, just out of boot camp, and stationed aboard a submarine at Pearl Harbor. Dirk was handsome but, more than that, he was funny, outgoing, and friendly. I had a crush on him from the moment I saw him, and so did a lot of other girls at our church. He was easy to like. Since Dirk did not have a car, I drove him to church and the singles' activities along with his roommates. It became clear pretty quickly that he had a crush on me, too. Before long, he asked me out on a date.

Dirk and I met on a Saturday afternoon for our first date. I was nervous but mostly excited. We had agreed on hiking in Sacred Falls State Park. I liked that he was adventurous and outdoorsy, and didn't mind a 4.2-mile hike on his day off! We talked the entire distance about our families, living in Hawaii, and the beauty of God's creation. He was easy to talk to, and I felt very at ease with him, even though we still barely knew each other. As we walked the dry dirt trail on a steep section, my foot slid, and I fell in the dirt. I was not hurt, but I was embarrassed. I was trying to make a good impression, after all! As Dirk helped me up, laughing, I brushed the dust off my shorts and began to laugh, too.

But I wasn't alone in feeling like a klutz. A bit later, the trail narrowed, and we had to walk single file. Dirk went first and kept looking back to talk to me. At one point, as he turned back around, he walked right into a tree branch and was nearly knocked to the ground. He put his hand to his forehead, rubbing where the limb had poked him, and exclaimed, "Ouch!" I laughed as I said, "That's what you get for laughing at me!" With that, any ice was well and truly broken. We spent the rest of the hike laughing together.

At the top of the hike, we arrived in a clearing where a beautiful waterfall roared down over the rocks. Everything was damp and mossy. A few other people swam in the pool there, diving under the falls, but we sat on a large rock together instead and continued talking. I told him one of the Hawaiian legends of Sacred Falls. Dirk shared that he still felt out of place in Hawaii; it was so different from anywhere else he'd ever lived. With that in mind, I suggested grabbing dinner at McDonald's after our hike. Dirk got a regular burger and fries, but I ordered a teriyaki burger with strawberry-guava juice. Dirk may still have felt out of place in Hawaii, but I loved everything about it. I knew I could have lived there happily forever.

After that, Dirk and I got serious fairly quickly. He asked me out anytime he was free, and I gladly said yes. We had a lot of fun together; I was excited to share my faith with him—one of my essential requirements for a future spouse. Dirk and I began to hang out with another couple, James and Penny, double dating and spending time at Penny's parents' home, which was near our church. Together, we played laser tag and mini-golf, went bowling, and on more hikes. We spent sunny afternoons and watched sunsets on the beach. Dirk continued to get plenty of attention from other girls, but he only had eyes for me. It made me feel special that such a handsome, charming guy was all mine.

Every few days, Dirk would have a twenty-four-hour duty on board his submarine. Instead of skipping a chance to see each other, I would pack a picnic dinner, and meet him at the pier. We sat side by side with our feet hanging off the front, eating and chatting. I was beginning to see Dirk and I having a future together.

Of course, not everything was perfect between us. We had a few fights. One Saturday afternoon, I met an old guy friend from college at a local diner. He was only in town for a few days, and it was nice to catch up. Dirk wasn't happy about me having lunch with another guy, despite my assurances that we had only ever been friends. During my lunch, Dirk called me repeatedly, crying and telling me that he loved me, but insisting that I was betraying him. I told him I was having lunch and would meet him back at Penny's parents' house later on.

When I got to Penny's house, her mom took me into her bedroom privately to tell me how devastated Dirk had been. I didn't understand how having lunch with an old friend could spark such a huge reaction, but I apologized to Dirk for hurting his feelings. I didn't think any more about it, but Dirk brought it up several more times, especially when I couldn't meet him because of parent-teacher meetings, school concerts, or other work obligations. I reminded him that my job as a teacher comes with expectations to attend all the school functions. I could lose my position if I missed them; he finally agreed to let it go.

A few nights later, Dirk called with a problem. His supervisor had ordered him to have his pay direct deposited. But Dirk did not get to the bank before it closed. Besides, he confided, he did not know how to open a bank account; he had never had money to put in one before. Begging me for help, he suggested I let him deposit his pay to my bank account. I didn't feel comfortable with that. After all, what if we broke up? What would happen then? I didn't like the idea of co-mingling finances with anyone. But Dirk brushed aside my concerns. "We're dating, and it's getting serious. I'm sure it will be fine," was his reasoning. I didn't want Dirk to get into trouble or feel bad, so, somehow, I found myself reluctantly agreeing.

We faithfully attended the weekly singles' church group Bible study. The leader frequently discussed sexual purity. He stressed, "Now to the unmarried … if they cannot control themselves, they should marry: for it is better to marry than to burn with passion," (I Corinthians 7:8-9 NIV). To keep ourselves pure from sexual sins, he advised dating only for a short time with the purpose of courtship. He reminded us that courtship is a time when a couple gets to know one another and decides if there will be an engagement. I had never thought about courtship or having a short engagement. Everyone I knew was engaged for at least a year, and the families had met and approved of the marriage.

After attending several of these Bible study sessions, Dirk shared that he was leaving on a six-month deployment. Having become familiar with military families, I had learned that fiancés got no information or support, but wives got all the information, communications, and support from the command. I wanted to avoid sexual temptation, and neither Dirk nor I wanted the lack of communication. We started to talk seriously about getting married.

A few weeks later, Dirk asked if he could come to my apartment to make a special dinner for us. "Of course," I said. When I picked him up, he had a bag full of groceries.

Arriving at my place, he went to the kitchen right away and began to cook. The minute he asked where to find different pans or utensils, I tried to go to the kitchen to show him, but he said, "No, just tell me." He wanted me to be surprised.

We had planned to eat on the couch and watch *The Princess Bride*, a favorite of both of ours. When he finished cooking, he plated our meals and brought them out to the living room. I noticed his hands were shaking. Just then, he tipped my plate a bit too far downward. The spaghetti slid off the plate and onto my light gray carpeting with a "splat." Embarrassed, he repeatedly apologized as he cleaned up the spaghetti and scrubbed the spot with a carpet cleaner to ensure the sauce would not leave a stain. He looked so sweet and nervous that I had to stifle a giggle. I didn't want him to feel any worse than he already did.

Dirk made me another plate of spaghetti, making sure not to spill it, and we watched the movie. At the end of the film, Dirk leaned over next to me on the couch and asked me to marry him. I said, "Yes."

4. THE WEDDING

"[Love]beareth all things, believeth all things, hopeth all things, endureth all things." – I Corinthians 13:7 KJV

As the wedding approached, Dirk spent more and more time at my apartment. We talked about our future together, my teaching job and his Navy career, and the possibility of having children. We agreed to keep the condominium where I was living since it was close to my teaching job. Dirk was going on deployment anyway. When I went home for Christmas break to prepare for our wedding, he moved his belongings into my apartment.

On Christmas Eve, Dirk called me. "I almost died today, but don't worry, I'm okay," was his first statement. I was shocked as he explained that he had taken a new shipmate to a local spot where people climb up a twenty-five-foot rock outcropping known as "Jump Rock" to plummet into Waimea Bay below. As part of the mission team, I had experienced the thrill of stepping off the rock while counting to ten before I splashed into the clear blue water. The church teen group who had taken us to Waimea Bay warned us to cross our ankles and fold our arms across our chest to avoid a bathing suit "malfunction" when hitting the water. The jump was intense. What an adrenaline rush!

All the locals knew about those big waves that come in December, but Dirk was unfamiliar with the fact that Hawaiian oceanographers measure waves from the back, not the crest as they do on the U.S. mainland. The big waves routinely reach heights of thirty or more feet with deadly undertows and rip tides, especially during the Pacific Ocean winter storm season, which comes in December and January. I loved sitting on Waimea Beach, listening to those big waves and watching their fury. I could feel God's power in the forcefulness of the waves shaking the earth as they broke on the shore.

Dirk and his friend had ignored both the rip current and the signs warning that no lifeguards were on duty. Once they climbed Jump Rock, Dirk leaped from the rock outcropping and, upon hitting the water, he got caught in the undertow and rip current. He was quite emotional as he relayed how his body was subsequently tumbled and pummeled by the sand and water until he finally crawled to the shore exhausted.

I was relieved to know that God had kept him safe, but I questioned his lack of judgment. I had always loved sitting on Waimea Beach, listening to those big waves, and watching their fury. I could feel God's power in the forcefulness of the waves shaking the earth as they broke on the shore. Those waves were no joke. I was so worried—why hadn't he paid attention to the warnings? Dirk dismissed my concerns as a lesson learned. "I can handle it," he assured me.

Back at home, I was deeply involved in final wedding preparations—ordering the wedding cake, checking with the florist, fittings for wedding gown alterations and arranging hair salon and manicure appointments--and preparing for Dirk's arrival.

When he and his family finally arrived, they stayed with my family. The nearest hotel was over thirty minutes away, and they didn't have money for an extended stay at a hotel.

The wedding ceremony was very short. A couple from my parents' church sang, then their minister gave a short message about love and marriage before we exchanged rings. My parents insisted that, even though Dirk did not have any money, I needed both an engagement ring and a wedding ring. He picked a diamond chip engagement ring with a matching ten-carat gold wedding band. It was all we could afford.

A family friend who had taken dozens of pictures of my

brother and me from the time we were born was our wedding photographer. This man had a pronounced German accent and, as he excitedly tried to explain where we were to position ourselves for the photos, Dirk did not understand his directions. Since I had known him for years, I knew he was saying, "Just the bride." Dirk thought he was saying, "Kiss the bride," and was delighted to oblige! Finally, I got my pictures by myself, and we headed to the reception in the church fellowship hall.

After we had a chance to cut the cake, greet all of our guests, and take a few more pictures, I changed into a traveling outfit for our drive to Niagara Falls where we would honeymoon.

Our guests threw small cups of birdseed as we left the church. I turned to say thank you to my bridesmaid and matron of honor just as they tossed large handfuls of birdseed, most of which landed in my mouth. As we drove away from the church, I realized that birdseed had fallen in places that it should never be!

We stopped at a nearby car wash to scrape the toothpaste off the back window. It had been used to announce our marriage, but, as it was December, the now frozen toothpaste did not come off. However, I was able to run to the ladies' room and remove some of the birdseed from my unmentionables.

We needed to drive several hours to Niagara Falls from the church. After a short time, Dirk pulled over in a rest area. I didn't know why at first, but he said that since we were married, he could not wait any longer. He rationalized that oral sex would care for his physical needs. It would "tide him over" until we reached the hotel room. "Shouldn't a wife take care of her husband's needs?" he rationalized.

My mind screamed: *I can't do that in a car!* "What if someone sees us?" I asked hesitantly.

"People will see the "Just Married" on the car and not pay any attention to us," he sweet-talked, so I complied with his wishes. After all, wasn't I supposed to obey my husband now that we were married?

At the hotel in Niagara Falls, I opened my suitcase only to find more birdseed! I burst into giggles. I felt as if I needed to apologize to the hotel maid for the mess.

I was excited to see the sights nearby or go on a hike, just like we did at home in Hawaii, but Dirk didn't want to leave the hotel room, saying, "I can't get enough of you." But I was now sore and hurt all over from what I considered his unnecessary roughness.

Dirk only agreed to go out when he got hungry. After breakfast, we walked along from our hotel to the Guinness Book of World Records Museum. After browsing through the exhibits, we continued walking along the edge of the Falls.

I thought the scenery was beautiful, frozen, glittery, and shining in the sunlight. The constant mist coated the trees, grass, and even the railings in ice. As we walked, I held Dirk's arm. He said his mother instilled in him how to treat a lady. She never opened her car door but instead would wait for him to open her door before getting out. I hoped he would always do the same for me. I liked his opening doors for me and walking with my arm in his arm.

A bit further down the sidewalk, I slipped on a particularly icy spot and gripped Dirk's arm to regain my balance. He steadied me, scolding, "You almost pulled me down."

"I apologize," I said. "Thank you for helping me catch my balance."

5. IT BEGINS

"Husbands, love your wives, even as Christ also loved the church, and gave himself for it."
— Ephesians 5:25 KJV

Arriving back in Hawaii after our New Year's honeymoon, I had to face the reality that Dirk was going to sea on a submarine for six months. He would leave in the next month.

The Navy chaplain conducted pre-deployment meetings for the crew and their families to discuss the emotional stages of a six-month or longer deployment. As he spoke, I could identify some of the steps in my feelings.

The first stage is anticipation, knowing the deployment is coming and dreading it, but having to prepare for his absence. Simple tasks like watching him pack, making sure he had enough toiletries and snacks, were more emotional than I had anticipated. I thought that, since we were newly married, I wouldn't miss him as much. Now I was missing him before he was even gone, and learning that these feelings were to be expected.

The second stage is detachment and withdrawal as Dirk was getting ready to leave. He worked long hours and seemed like he was prepared. I felt that if he had to go, he should just get it over with and leave already. I was in that phase: check.

The third stage is a complete disruption, which happens when the ship leaves. All the things I did with Dirk, dinner together after work, picnics on the pier, waking up to him calling me pretty, smart, and sexy, were gone. My house seemed empty with just me and my cats.

While Dirk was on deployment, I spent more quality time with my cat. I poured myself into my Christian school teaching ministry. I arrived at work early and came home late. On Thursday afternoons, grades five and six teachers would order pizza and stay at work late. I enjoyed having people to talk to; I was afraid of the day my cat would speak back to me in English. Getting together with the other teachers or Navy wives was also a pleasant diversion. Anything to keep me from wondering if Dirk was okay and thinking about all of the things that could go wrong on a submarine.

I prayed daily that God would help me to keep trusting Him as much as I did when He sent the money for me to go on the mission trip. The Holy Spirit reminded me that nothing could keep God from loving and caring for us. "For I am persuaded, that neither death nor life, nor angels nor principalities, nor powers, nor things present nor things to come, nor height nor depth, nor any other creature, shall be able to separate us from the love of God which is in Christ Jesus our Lord," (Romans 8:38, 39 KJV). Even submarines!

Some of the other Navy wives liked to scrapbook and make greeting cards. I thought that might be fun. I was invited to a scrapbook party and became enamored with all the accessories. I found a new hobby.

Christy, one of the other "single" navy wives, hosted scrapbook and card parties at her home on Saturday nights. We called ourselves "single" navy wives because we were by ourselves while our husbands were deployed, and we had no children. We spent many Saturday nights sharing stories, scissors, pictures, and cardstock paper. We helped each other through the lonely lack of communication. After all, we were "in the same boat," so to speak, much like our husbands were.

Navy communications with submarines on deployment back then were called Family Grams. Limited to less than fifty words, they were heavily censored and sent and received only during specific operational periods. I could have no messages for weeks. Then when the schedule indicated the submarine could pull into a port, I would sit by my phone, hoping I could hear Dirk's voice or get an email or postcard.

When Dirk was able to call, we talked as long as possible. He said he was writing "fantasies" about me expressing all the things he wanted to do with me sexually. I was extremely uncomfortable with this topic, even with my husband, but Dirk was relentless in discussing it. He had written over one hundred pages of these fantasies in a black marble composition notebook. I was dumbfounded. I didn't know what to say.

Dirk wanted me to write those same types of images back to him, but I couldn't. The thought of doing so was against all that I had learned from the Bible. Good girls didn't think and talk about that stuff all the time, did they? But Dirk wasn't put off by my refusals; instead, he badgered me constantly and quoted, "Marriage is honorable in all, and the bed undefiled," (Hebrews 13:4 KJV). I finally gave in and wrote a couple of Harlequin-style romance scenes. My fantasies were romantic, tender, and gentle. Dirk's were rough and dark and designed to shock me. We were clearly on very different pages. Dirk was never satisfied with my loving scenes.

The last two stages of a sailor's leave are homecoming and reintegration. When the day came for the submarine to return from deployment, the other wives, children, and friends and I all gathered on the pier. We happily waved "Welcome Home" signs and banners. Everyone was dressed up; some women even wore high heels. My practical side won over, realizing that I would probably trip and embarrass myself. I didn't want that on my husband's first return from deployment. I wore a new flowered dress, curled my hair, and made sure my makeup was just right. I even bought him a flower lei, in the Hawaiian tradition. It was the first time I had seen my husband in six months.

Around the halfway point of the six-month deployment, both the crew on the submarine and the family support group held night parties halfway. At the party, the Navy family support group had raffled off "First Kiss" tickets. The winner's husband got to be the first off the ship to kiss his wife. I was happy for my friend, Rachel, who won. After her husband, I watched as the captain, executive officer, and other crewmen got off the ship with enthusiastic smiles and into the waiting open arms of their families for excited hugs and kisses.

Finally, I spotted Dirk. I'm sure my face glowed. I was so happy to see him. He practically ran over people trying to get to me. We hugged and kissed, and then Dirk told me he only had a minute to say hello before he had to go back to finish his cleaning and packing. I tried to wait patiently, but it seemed to take him forever as I stood there on the pier waiting for him.

Dirk was anxious to get me home. He expected me to fulfill every one of the fantasies in his one hundred pages—including in public places—but I could not.

As we arrived home, Dirk picked me up and carried me through the back door, around the corner of the laundry and utility room, and into the living room where he placed me on the couch. He sat next to me with his arms around me, saying, "I dreamed of being home to hold you." His words were exactly what I needed to hear, except after a few minutes, I couldn't help saying, "Dirk, what is that smell?" He replied, "Oh, the submarine makes its own air and recycles it when we are underway." He didn't notice it at all. Boat smell can be best described as a "men's locker room with no heat or air conditioning, with a bit of a chemical touch added in.

Dirk said he was looking forward to taking a long hot shower since showers on the submarine were required to be five minutes or less. I suggested that while he showered I would throw his uniforms in the washing machine and make dinner. I was so happy to have him home.

I wanted to make my husband happy, but the things he was asking me to do felt way too uncomfortable. I felt dirty and guilty but conflicted. I didn't want to do what he was asking, but we were married, and I had vowed to "love, honor, and obey" my husband. *Shouldn't I please him?*

A day or two after Dirk's homecoming, I began to itch. My doctor diagnosed me with pubic lice! Although he had visited ports in southeast Asia where STD's are common, Dirk assured me that the man with whom he "hot racked" had infected him. According to Navy jargon, which I was still learning, "hot racking" is when two men take turns sleeping in a bunk aboard a ship. When one man is on duty, the other is sleeping in the bed, and vice-versa. Dirk apologized, and, naively, I believed him. Crying tears of humiliation, I used the medicine from the doctor.

Since they had recently returned after being away for so long, the captain gave his crew several days off. On one of these days off, Dirk took me to a local botanical garden where he sought out a bench and promptly sat down. I had brought my camera to take pictures of the stunning tropical plants and flowers. I expected to sit next to him, taking a few snapshots of us amid the tropical scenery, holding hands, talking about our future, and admiring God's beautiful creation.

Dirk had other plans. He desired a physical relationship. Forcefully, he pulled me down on his lap, pushed my underwear aside, and played out his fantasy. I felt mortified! How could we be so physical in such a public place?

I didn't dare cry out or make a scene as that would just draw attention to what we were doing. Dirk tried to calm my fears by assuring me that no one had noticed, and I was just so beautiful that he couldn't help himself. I didn't know whether to be flattered by all his attention or embarrassed.

Despite our issues around sex, I was happy to have Dirk home, joining me at all the church and school events. The church picnic came around and with it the anniversary of the first time we met. He showed off his skateboard flips and tricks with some of the other guys. I pleasantly chatted with the women as we arranged the picnic buffet tables, adjusting each bowl so that people could reach the deliciousness from both sides of the buffet table lines.

As we talked, some of the other ladies brought up the subject of husbands and the old saying, "Boys don't grow up, only their toys get bigger." I agreed, pointing over to Dirk doing tricks on his skateboard. We all laughed at that, and I didn't think anything more about it. The women were in charge of the food, but the men were in charge of the games. Both the food and games were good at the picnic; it seemed everyone had a great time.

Back at our condo, I was happily relating several of the lovely conversations, and what I thought was an enjoyable day. However, I paused when Dirk's face tightened as if in anger as I told the joke about "big boys and their toys" and pointing to him on his skateboard as an example. *Why?* I wondered, *What happened?*

Dirk was furious. He did not see the humor in that old saying. He thought that when I referred to him on his skateboard, it was the same as calling him a child in front of the other ladies. In his opinion, I had wholly embarrassed and betrayed him. I didn't understand why he was upset. It was supposed to be a joke, just harmless teasing among friends.

I had never seen him or anyone so angry. I was afraid.

"Who said that?" he demanded,

"I don't remember," I defended. I could not understand why Dirk was livid.

"Who?" he badgered. He would not let the subject go; I was frightened. I had never seen anyone that upset before. "I think it was the pastor's wife who started the conversation," I said, but I wasn't sure who began the conversation. I only remembered that I had agreed and pointed at my husband as an example.

"Where are you going?" I questioned as Dirk grabbed the car keys.

"To straighten this out and explain that I'm not a boy!" He slammed the door as he left.

I didn't know what to do with myself. My husband had gone to confront the pastor's wife! I was in trouble. The only thing I knew to do was kneel by my bed in tears to ask God for help. I poured my heart out to God. I begged God's forgiveness for making my husband upset and prayed that Dirk would come back in a calm state so that we could talk things out.

After about an hour, he returned. With tear-stained eyes, I met him at the door. He glared at me. "You did it! The pastor's wife told me. You embarrassed me; I went over there to set her straight, and it was you the whole time." I tried to defend myself. "It was a joke, and you were doing tricks on your skateboard. I didn't mean to embarrass you."

I hung my head in shame. I was sorry. I didn't know he would confront her. I thought downplaying it would diffuse the situation. I had forgotten the verses I had memorized in high school: "Put on, therefore, as the elect of God, holy and beloved...kindness, humbleness of mind, meekness, longsuffering;" (Colossians 3:12 KJV). Dirk did not speak to me for a day or two after that. He went to work for his twenty-four-hour shift and did not call home.

While Dirk was at work, I called to apologize to the pastor's wife for using Dirk as an example and joke in the "boys and their toys" conversation. I asked her for forgiveness. I vowed to trust God to help me better understand my husband and dismissed this incident as a newlywed misunderstanding. Dirk finally accepted my apology and took me out for a picnic lunch at the beach park in Waikiki. We had made up, and life was good.

Except Dirk's sexual fantasies continued. One evening we went to the beach after sunset. I laid out a towel, hoping we could listen to the surf, watch the stars, and talk about everything and anything. I wanted to catch him up on all that he had missed during his six months at sea.

Despite my protests, he pulled me down onto the sand, purposely leaving marks on my chest and neck, saying, "These prove that I own your body." He could do anything to me at any time he wanted. At first, I thought his attention and possessiveness was romantic. It was flattering how beautiful he thought I was. And it was, I assumed, much better to be wanted by your husband all the time than to have an indifferent husband!

Our first anniversary was coming up, so Dirk asked for vacation time at Christmas, and his commanding officer granted his request. We flew off to meet Dirk's family.

Christmas meant a lot to me growing up. There were lots of happy traditions such as attending the Candlelight Christmas Eve Service together, making cookies to eat after the Christmas Eve Service, and plenty of gatherings with our large, loving family.

Dirk's family was far different. Christmas reminded them of all they could not afford. I did not understand all the stress and unhappiness. We stayed with his mom and sister in their small apartment and helped decorate their tree while our cat played hide and seek, peeking out between the branches to swat the ornaments as we hung them.

After decorating the Christmas tree, we put on a movie. I asked if I could get anyone else a drink since I was getting up to get myself one. As I turned to walk to the kitchen, Dirk swept my feet out from under me. When I landed hard on the carpeted concrete floor, he laughed. "You should have seen the look on your face," he howled in delight.

I began to cry. I hurt!

Dirk pulled me onto his lap in a feeble gesture of apology. My voice shaky, I asked, "Why would you do such a thing?"

"I thought it would be funny."

"It was not funny. You hurt me!" I cried.

He hugged me but did not attempt to apologize further.

The next morning after my shower, I noticed a large bruise where I had landed. I couldn't believe the man who loved me could hurt me like that.

Little did I know.

6. NEW ENGLAND

"The steps of a good man are ordered by the Lord: and he delighteth in his way." – Psalm 37:23 KJV

I was full of mixed emotions leaving Hawaii. I had met my husband there. I would miss my church and school teacher friends, along with the warm weather, but I was excited to go someplace that I had never been. Besides, Dirk's submarine was being decommissioned, so the whole crew was moving, not just us. Most of my Navy wife friends and their families would be moving along with me.

The submarine transferred from Hawaii to Maine and was due to arrive in February. The families gathered on the pier once again to watch as the boat sailed away, but this time everyone was quiet. Some of the wives wiped away tears as they watched their husbands walk down the pier, board the ship, and disappear down the ladder. Even when we knew we would see them again, saying good-bye was painful.

The movers put everything we owned in boxes and loaded them into a truck. It felt strange and a bit uncomfortable to watch as people took my clothes out of the closet and dresser to put in boxes. All the towels, dishes, and even the contents of my desk were boxed and packed in the truck.

Cammie, a fellow Navy wife and church member, had warned me about her bad experience with the movers. When they'd broken the seal on the container with all their household goods, they couldn't believe the offensive stench! As the movers unloaded the boxes, Cammie and her husband, Greg, tried to air out the couch and mattress. As the truck emptied, they found the source-- a full diaper genie had been packed in the container and shipped from Connecticut to Hawaii in the heat of summer. The stink of the dirty diapers was nauseating; she remembered it quite vividly.

I had made sure all the trash cans were empty and my cat was in his kennel so he did not get out or get packed in the truck. Those stories were an urban legend, and I wanted no part of being that type of legendary.

I signed the official papers saying that the container was shut and sealed with stickers. Our household goods, as the Navy had labeled them, would be delivered to our new place in Maine. I would have to sign those same papers again when my boxes were delivered. I realized that I needed to trust God to take care of my earthly possessions, and I said a quick, silent prayer as the truck drove away.

The next day, I flew home to spend some time with my parents, who met me at the airport with a winter coat. We stopped at a store on the way home specifically for me to buy some warm socks. In Hawaii, where I'd lived for the last six years, socks were only worn with tennis shoes and then not very often. I only wore sandals, flip-flops, or "slippers" as they called them. I also had to retrieve my sweaters and long pants from storage. New England was cold, especially in December, and I was used to the warm, tropical Hawaiian sunshine.

After spending a few days relaxing at my parents' house, I needed to go to my new home to get everything ready for Dirk's arrival. His submarine was scheduled to arrive soon, and I was excited to welcome him to our new home.

The wives and families were not allowed to wait on the pier; a snowstorm was approaching, and the wind was causing negative temperatures. It was a vast difference from the welcome home gatherings on the dock in Hawaii. We waited at the Navy recreation center in a big meeting room. It was warm, and our husbands would be driven to meet us there. Dirk was one of the last to arrive--again. But I didn't care. I was happy to have him home. Plus, being part of a decommissioning crew meant that he would not go out to sea for a while and would have more time off.

I had unpacked and set up the house before Dirk arrived. He contentedly let me give him the tour of our small two-bedroom apartment. At first, our Navy housing condominium seemed very, very cold. The housing manager seemed annoyed when I asked to have someone check our heating system. "You people spent too much time in Hawaii; you'll get used to it," he said sharply.

After repeated phone calls, a repair technician finally came to check our heating system. The technician found a problem with the thermostat mechanism. With a fifty-degree setting, the heat only came on when the temperature of our house dropped below that point. The repairman apologized and fixed it right away. It turned out that I wasn't just overly sensitive from living in Hawaii for too long!

Dirk offered to hang our pictures on the wall, and I got him the hammer and the measuring tape. He wanted to be sure the photos were level on the wall. I watched him measure from the ceiling where the top corner of the large picture would hang over our couch. Then he hammered the nail into the wall and hung the picture on it. We stepped back to look at it. It was nowhere near level. Dirk measured each corner to the ceiling again. No, he had not made a measuring error. The roof in our apartment was not level, and the edges were not square. We ended up just leveling the pictures with a small level.

We found a small Baptist church in the town where we lived. The pastor and his wife were an older couple with a high school-aged daughter. The sanctuary windows overlooked the parsonage with a direct view of the pastor's vegetable garden. I will never forget the Sunday morning message that was interrupted by the minister saying, "I'm sorry, I can't keep my train of thought. A deer is eating the vegetables from my garden." From the pulpit, he explained that he would install some scarecrows or a fence so the wildlife could not distract him—or eat his garden.

Our small church helped to support missionaries in Australia. One Sunday afternoon after the morning service and fellowship dinner, the missionary speaker asked if someone would like to try "Australia food." Dirk readily volunteered, and the missionary instructed him to "open wide." I watched, trying not to laugh, as Dirk tasted a big spoonful of vegemite, a thick, dark brown spread made from leftover brewers' yeast extract with various vegetable and spice additives. He sputtered, "It's awful!"

I knew that moving from Hawaii to New England during the winter months would be challenging, but it wasn't just the cold that made me uncomfortable. I developed allergy-induced asthma. I could barely breathe at times, and it seemed as if arms were encircling me and squeezing me to death. Navy doctors conducted tests to determine I had allergies and asthma. Specifically, I was most allergic to willow trees, birch trees, maple trees, and almost every type of evergreen tree you could think of to use as a Christmas tree, except Douglas Fir. I was even allergic to the grass in my yard. Even if I was wearing shoes, if my feet and ankles happened to pick up any grass clippings, I would get all red and itchy wherever it touched. It was terrible. I felt like I was allergic to every green plant or tree in New England, and that doesn't even count the indoor things like dust and mold that triggered my asthma. I carried my inhaler in my purse when I went out or kept it nearby when I was at home. The allergist recommended that I begin taking medication and weekly allergy shots.

Dirk, on the other hand, really loved the change from Hawaii to Maine. He had more time off since he was not at sea. Of course, to him, all of the downtimes meant more time to have all his fantasies fulfilled. Not feeling well, I tried to talk him out of them, but, in the end, I always gave in. I hoped someday he would be satisfied, but that hope seemed impossible with his insatiability and insistence on fulfilling his fantasies. Unfortunately, I didn't see that changing anytime soon. I closed the drapes in hopes the neighbors didn't hear or see anything.

We made friends with another younger couple who attended our church and lived down the street from us. They, too, were newly married with a baby boy. Hilary, the wife, and I became friends. We talked about taking care of our homes, gardening, and cooking. We traded frugal recipes for meals, and she taught me how to make my own cleaning supplies, seeing that neither of our husbands made much money. I didn't even know there was such a thing as a recipe for a spray glass cleaner or laundry detergent.

Hilary stayed at home with their baby, but I found a job as a bank teller in a nearby town. It paid a little over minimum wage, but it gave me something to do and gave us a little extra spending money.

Dirk walked or biked to work each day and would stop to pick wildflowers to bring home to me. It was sweet. I started a small ceramic lighthouse collection. To me, they showed God's message: "The Lord is my light and my salvation, whom shall I fear?" (Psalm 27:1 KJV). I packed a picnic lunch, and we spent many happy afternoons at the lighthouse taking pictures of the tower with the waves breaking on the rocky New England shore and walking the trail next to the water.

We saved up our money and bought in-line skates, along with helmets and pads. Dirk had skated all his life, but I had never used in-line roller skates. I told Dirk about the church roller skating parties I attended in high school, but this was all new. I wondered if it was going to be like ice skating, as I put on the skates sitting at our tiny kitchen table.

When I stood up, I rolled halfway across the floor. I stopped moving as I grabbed the kitchen counter. It turns out that the foundation of our apartment was not level either. So, I used the table, the wall and door frame to get outside onto the sidewalk and street.

I only had one difficulty. Ice skates have a toe pick, and I was used to pushing off of it. Inline skates have a break in the back. The first time I tried to push off the (nonexistent) toe pic, I lost my balance and did what resembled a twirl. We laughed together. Dirk and I had great fun skating around our neighborhood, down a small hill to the tennis courts, laughing, and enjoying the springtime. The way home was not quite as pleasant; it was mostly uphill.

I wondered what God thought about our marriage. Being a "good Christian wife" meant pleasing my husband. I tried to ignore my conscience and go along with Dirk's wishes. But watching the pastor and his wife work together, I pondered, *Is this how God expects a Christian marriage to function?*

Watching the tenderness and patience Hilary and her husband had for each other and the natural, loving way the pastor and his wife worked together, I began to question whether or not our marriage was the way God wanted a Christian marriage to function. *Was there something wrong?*

7. CONTINUATION

"Who can find a virtuous woman? For her price is far above rubies. The heart of her husband doth safely trust in her so that he shall have no need of spoil. She will do him good and not evil all the days of her life." — Proverbs 31:10-12 KJV

After the two seemingly short years of living in Maine, the Navy reassigned Dirk to a submarine homeported in Norfolk, Virginia, that was frequently out to sea. Once we arrived and found an apartment, I sought out a church that we could attend that also had a Christian school. I started teaching part-time in the Christian school and taking classes in the seminary for a graduate degree in religious education. I was thrilled to be back in God's service.

I met a fellow Navy wife at church who shared that her youngest son was deaf. As we became friends, she taught me American Sign Language (ASL). Since they were in charge of the deaf ministry, I joined them. They were the interpreters for every church service. To give them a small reprieve, I began by signing the closing hymn and invitation. I joined the church choir. I was happily involved in the church and school ministries. Dirk even joined the deaf ministry with me. I was thrilled to be able to be in God's service wherever He sent us. I was making friends, and it wasn't long before I felt almost as at home as I had in Hawaii.

We didn't live far from my grandparents. We visited them often. We walked in the local botanical garden and continued our tradition of picnic meals on the pier while Dirk was on twenty-four-hour duty. We bought season passes to the local amusement and water park. It was so much fun to ride the roller coasters and water slides on our days off.

Life at home on the other hand, was decidedly less pleasant. Dirk's fantasies and ideas for sex games became darker and more perverse. He tied me to the bedposts and would leave money by the bed when I awoke the next morning as if I were a prostitute. I felt degraded and humiliated. I cried myself to sleep more nights than I could count.

Why would he treat me this way? Convinced I needed to follow my Bible teaching, I submitted to my husband; it was Biblical teaching. I didn't have a choice. Disturbed by my husband's fantasies and desires, I prayed that God would give me peace and help me every night and every morning. I enrolled in a "Proverbs 31 Woman" course as part of my degree program. The professor's teachings made the verses relevant to our lives as modern Christian women, wives, and mothers. I felt her teachings inspired me to become a better Christian woman and wife. Little did I know that her inspiration would come back to haunt me later.

While I was happily involved in serving God in the Christian school and seminary, Dirk went to sea for short one- and two-week cruises aboard his submarine. After one of these quick deployments, Dirk shared that he was sore. As his wife, I wondered what would cause his genital blisters. He explained away the problem saying he masturbated very frequently. He could not help himself; he missed me so much. He compared his blisters to the blisters on your feet from new shoes that rub on your heels the wrong way. I naively accepted his explanation, and life continued. I quickly pushed away any other thoughts from my mind. I was married to him, so I needed to meet his frequent daily needs— whatever they were. I prayed that God would help me.

∞

Later that year, I finished my Master of Religious Education degree program and graduated with honors. I received the vocal music award and wore my medal at graduation. I was proud of myself and excited for what this could mean for my career.

Everything was going so well except for in the bedroom. No one knew of my internal struggle; I had confided in no one—not even my mom or my closest friends. I desperately wanted to be a good Christian wife, but I felt guilty about submitting to Dirk's sexual fantasies. I knew God cared about everyone and saw everything involving His children. But I couldn't understand why I felt so degraded if our marriage was indeed a Biblical one. I kept asking, *Is this part of Your plan for my marriage?*

8. BACK TO HAWAII

"And Jesus called a little child unto him, and set him in the midst of them, And said, Verily I say unto you, except ye be converted, and become as little children, ye shall not enter into the kingdom of heaven." – Matthew 18:2-3

A few months later, Dirk and I said goodbye to Virginia. Again, I felt sad to leave the friends I had made, but I was pleasantly surprised that the Navy had reassigned him to Hawaii. I was glad to return and arranged an interview with the principal at my former school. If I could teach there again, I would be in heaven!

Arriving back in Hawaii felt as if I were coming home. I loved the people at our church, the Christian school, and the Navy wives' group. I could hardly wait to jump back into all the activities.

My interview at the Christian school went very well, and I was hired for a teaching job—first grade. Although I was reluctant to take on first graders, I met with the previous teacher who explained the curriculum and materials. I became convinced that God was placing me where He wanted me.

I was assigned the gifted and talented students—twelve boys and six girls—all of whom were enthusiastic about learning. It was better than I could have expected. The children asked for difficult spelling words like the names of dinosaurs—stegosaurus and tyrannosaurus. They cheered over learning to spell everyday items such as banana and umbrella. After we whizzed through the addition and subtraction materials, the students asked to learn their multiplication tables. Their Bible verse memorization and catechism recitations were spot-on. They were a joy to teach.

Dirk and I began enjoying all the things we used to do in Hawaii. We went hiking, walking on the beach, and window shopping in Waikiki, along with the young married couples' Bible study life group activities, and church and school functions kept us busy. I was happy.

After Christmas break, I began feeling ill. My monthly period unexpectedly started during class, and I had to excuse myself to change my clothes. I felt nauseous and dizzy. Since I was going to be out of work for several days, I made substitute teacher plans for my class.

I felt sure that I was not pregnant, but my cycle had never been this heavy and was usually over in four to five days. *It will be over soon,* I reasoned. However, what I thought did not happen. I continued to bleed for so long that a Navy wife friend who happened to come by with ice cream to cheer me up ended up putting the ice cream in the freezer and driving me to the Army hospital emergency room instead.

The doctors diagnosed *menorrhagia,* a flow so massive it can soak through an extra heavy flow pad in an hour; it can cause anemia and severe cramps. When an ultrasound confirmed a blood clot in my uterus that was slowly bleeding, the ER physician consulted with my primary care doctor. They discussed allowing it to continue evacuating naturally rather than surgically.

However, on day thirty of this seemingly endless cycle, I was still bleeding excessively. Dirk was out to sea on short one- and two-week deployments for most of this time. So, another friend, a colleague from the Christian school, stopped by my house and brought my students' papers to grade while I was recuperating. Then she watched in horror as I almost collapsed because of dizziness from anemia as I got up from the couch. She rushed me to the hospital.

We waited in the emergency room for triage until the nurse showed me into a room. The on-call doctor who interviewed me asked, "How long has this problem been going on?" His second question upset me. "Do you have any history of psychological issues?"

I retorted, "If you'd been bleeding for thirty days or more, you'd be having psychological issues, too. Now, call my doctor."

Fearful now that the blood clot could move to my heart, lungs, or brain, the on-call doctor planned immediate emergency surgery. When he stepped out of my room, I called a fellow church member who happened to be the hospital's head of the radiology department. He had read my MRIs, x-rays, and ultrasounds, and he determined that I was not in grave danger—contrary to the ER doctor's opinion.

The ER doctor was very unhappy with my going over his head, but he gave me fluids and sent me home with strict instructions to rest and avoid strenuous or sexual activity.

I was able to relax and prevent most taxing activity, but Dirk, being back from deployment for a week, said, "I can't control myself around you." So much for following the doctor's orders.

A few days later, I had my first gynecological surgery. After the surgery, I spent the night in the hospital. At my three-day postoperative appointment, the skeptical doctor told me that he had removed almost a half-liter of infection from my uterus. He was amazed that my body had miraculously "walled off the infection." He found no explanation for the disease during the surgery. Detailing the procedure, he commented, "You should have died from that quantity of infection in your body."

I told the doctor about my first-grade class of students in a Christian school who had been praying for me every morning. "God answered the children's prayers," I explained.

"Those children must have a lot of faith," he responded.

This conversation reminded me of Jesus, calling the children to him after His disciples had tried to send them away. "Unless you change and become like little children, you will not enter the kingdom of heaven," (Matthew 18:3 NIV). Jesus was reminding His disciples, and us in the present day, to come to Him with the simple faith of a child.

God had honored my students' trust and had answered their prayers. They made get well cards and had them delivered to me. The church ladies brought meals so I wouldn't have to cook. One family even brought me a chocolate French Silk Pie from my favorite restaurant. God was using His church people to take care of me while Dirk was in port and out to sea sporadically throughout all this turmoil.

The doctor ordered me to rest and recuperate with no sexual activity for six weeks after the surgery. I tried, but Dirk was so desperate. He waited three of the six weeks and then relentlessly forced himself on me, saying, "You look so sexy in bed. I can't restrain myself."

I was not sexy; I was ill. The specialists had never seen anything like what was wrong with me. I prayed that the bleeding would stop. I prayed that I would be able to carry a child someday, possibly even soon.

The doctors tried several gynecological procedures to stop the bleeding, none of which worked for long. At one point, the doctors administered a shot to induce menopause. The medication temporarily stopped the bleeding, but the side effects of hot flashes and mood swings were unbearable. Plus, Dirk assumed that I was "better" and demanded that I satisfy his needs. Finally, Dirk went on an extended deployment, and I had some time to recover.

However, I continued to bleed profusely. One morning, I called my pastor's wife to talk about my condition, and immediately she came to check on me. She was alarmed at my pale face and dizziness as I held onto the door. When I invited her inside, she picked up my purse and helped me get in her car. Off we went back to the emergency room.

When we arrived at the hospital, I remember thinking, *Wow! I don't even have to wait; I must be in bad shape.* The nurses took me to a private room and administered an IV. I went home several hours later to rest and wait for a medevac flight to San Diego. I needed to have yet another surgery and to meet a reproductive endocrinology specialist.

My mother met me in San Diego before the surgery. We had a couple of days to see the sights. We had a pleasant visit until I had to prepare for my surgery. The side effects of a fast or juice cleanse were minimal compared with the "surgical-prep" solutions I endured. The experience was horrendous!

After surgery and several days in the hospital, I was discharged and went to stay at my uncle's house. I was not allowed to fly home, and I needed someone to help me. I could not lift anything weighing more than a gallon of milk or walk more than a few steps without sitting down to rest. I wasn't allowed to drive either.

As I was out of work on disability for an extended period, my principal asked to meet with me about my teaching position. He surprised me by asking, "What will keep this from happening again? How do we know you will be able to finish out the school year? Can you assure me you will be okay?"

His lack of trust in God seemed evident to me from his questions. I answered, "There is no cure for what is wrong with me, and there is no precedent." Feeling defensive and a bit disrespectful, I persisted, "What's to keep you from being hit by a car tomorrow and breaking your leg? Only God knows what will happen tomorrow, and He has not chosen to tell any of us at this point."

Feeling my faith take hold, I continued, "God knows our future before we do, and He has promised, 'For I know the plans I have for you,' declares the Lord, 'plans to prosper you and not to harm you, plans to give you hope and a future,'" (Jeremiah 29:11 NIV).

I was insulted that the principal did not allow me to go back into my classroom as a teacher. He reasoned that I could be sick again, and the children needed "stability." Dirk suggested that we take the school to court; he, too, was angry at their absurd reasoning. They refused to allow me to teach because of the possibility that I could be sick again. Doesn't everyone have that same possibility at any time? I tried to reason with them, but there was no use arguing anymore. The administration had decided. Unless I quit, I would do as they asked.

These words of faith aside, the principal did not allow me to go back into my classroom as a teacher. I became a special assistant to the superintendent to coordinate our school accreditation visit. In advance of the accreditation team's visit to our school, I prepared all the paperwork, reserved hotel rooms, arranged meals, and classroom visits. I prayed that God would help me do my best, despite my resentment, and He helped change my attitude. The accreditation visit was a success. Our school gained the credential we had hoped for.

9. DIRK CHANGES

"Wives, submit yourselves unto your own husbands, as unto the Lord…Husbands, love your wives, even as Christ also loved the church, and gave himself for it."
— *Ephesians 5:22, 25 KJV*

I was glad to be back at work after being sick. It felt great to be able to get out of my house and to work for the Lord at the Christian school, even if I was not allowed back in the classroom. However, one afternoon I got a call from the command liaison of Dirk's submarine. Dirk had been taken off the ship in Guam and rushed to the Navy Hospital. The doctors were unsure of what had happened. He had lost about thirty pounds, was barely eating, sleeping all the time, and rarely communicating with anyone.

I was afraid; what could I do? The command would not allow me to fly to Guam. They assured me that he would get some rest at the hospital and be discharged in time to go back to sea with the rest of the crew. I had called Dirk's room and spoken to his doctor, who had ordered an MRI. I knew from talking with the Navy wives that if Dirk had an MRI, he would either have to drink or receive an injection with a radioactive chemical. He would not be allowed back for several weeks to give time for the dangerous chemical to leave his system. Otherwise, the radiation monitor he was required to wear would set off alarms on the ship.

The submarine left Guam as scheduled but without Dirk.

After being in the Navy hospital for almost two weeks with no definite diagnosis, Dirk was sent home on a MAC flight (Military Airlift Command) to recuperate. He went through security, customs, and medical clearances while I waited in the parking lot. The process took several hours, but I was thrilled to see him. I needed to hug Dirk to show him how much I missed him and prayed that he would get better.

Once back home, Dirk had several blood tests and doctor appointments. I was able to accompany him since he was not allowed to drive. The doctors diagnosed possible bacterial meningitis, but the test results were inconclusive. No one knew what had happened to Dirk.

His changes weren't just physical; I began to notice he had changed mentally, too. His personality had changed. He was unhappy, and had become much more serious. There was a lot less joking and teasing. He seemed critical of everything with no interest in doing all the things we had done before such as hiking, going to the beach, or hanging out with our church friends. I knew he stayed up late playing online computer games, but he became obsessed. It seemed he barely ate or slept after coming home from this mysterious illness. He sat at his computer for hours without a break. In fear of his relapsing into this mysterious illness, I began to bring him food and drinks at his computer workstation. As a good wife, I felt that I should take care of my sick husband. I couldn't get him to sleep, but at least I kept him hydrated.

Over lunch one afternoon, I begged him to talk to me about what had happened on that submarine. When had he started feeling sickly? Had he eaten something off? What had he been doing? Dirk said everything was normal, except that he and his team would mock wrestle in their time off. He spoke of their tournaments and being "thrown down." He showed me his hat, the one that he had been wearing when someone put staples into the bill of it as they were playing around, but nothing clearly explained why Dirk had become so ill.

Perplexed, I prayed to ask God to heal Dirk and to help me be the wife he needed. I knew that God would heal Dirk; after all, I believed, "Therefore I say unto you, what things soever ye desire when ye pray, believe that ye receive them, and ye shall have them," (Mark 11:24 KJV).

Dirk's health slowly returned, but his personality, the happy, fun-loving, outgoing man I had married, changed into someone I didn't know. He became secretive, demanding, more possessive, paranoid, even intimidating.

Dirk demanded that I tell him where I was going every time I left the house. He asked which friend I would see, what I was going to do, and how long I would be gone. Sometimes I was not allowed to leave the house. He began listening to my phone conversations to make sure I wouldn't betray him again like I had done in Hawaii when we were first married. Dirk pointed out that I needed to stay home to take care of him, emphasizing that taking care of my home was part of my Christian duty, just like the woman in Proverbs 31. After all, she took care of her house, and I should, too. Didn't I want to be a good Christian wife? He had touched on a nerve. I wanted to please God and be like the ideal Proverbs 31 woman; besides I didn't want to upset him or make things worse between us. So, I went along with it.

I didn't know what to do about Dirk's possessiveness; he was sure I was having an affair or something similar with someone on the internet. I knew God had healed Dirk's body. Perhaps Dirk needed more time for healing his spirit. As his wife, I tried to change my habits to appease him. I stayed home when he asked. I told him where I was going, with which female friends, and when I would return. I made his favorite foods for lunches and dinners. I picked up his favorite snacks and soda from the grocery store, making sure to keep them on hand. I wanted him to be happy and well, but I wasn't sure how to make it happen. I prayed that God would help me continue to be a good Christian woman and wife but wondered how He would answer my prayers.

10. HOPES DASHED

"Children are an heritage of the Lord: and the fruit of the womb is his reward." — Psalm 127:3 KJV

Dirk and I had good days when we could laugh and talk like when we were first married. He would get up from his spot at the computer, and we would watch comedy and adventure-type movies. After the movie, we would talk about having children. How many would we have? What would their names be? Dirk wanted three children, two boys, and a girl, and he had picked out their names when he was in high school. I wanted one or two children with names like Ashley Lauren or Justin Tyler. Dirk said the names I picked were "fancy." I replied, "Your cousins used the names you chose. We can't name our child the same as his or her cousin." Dirk wanted his daughter's name was to be Brooke and one of his sons to be named Ryan, and maybe the other would be Tony because of the great skateboarder, Tony Hawk. We agreed to disagree on the name debate since we thought we had a lot of time.

Our perception of the perfect family picture seemed incomplete. Dirk and I wanted to have children. We'd never tried to stop conception, but it had been years and still no baby. Consequently, we began the process of infertility screening. Dirk's results were low, but, in his opinion, I was the problem. I underwent several ultrasounds in the course of the treatments that led to the discovery of my bicornuate uterus. In laymen's terms, I had two uteri connected by a small passage. I had double periods, and my body was unable to stop the bleeding.

If I were ever to become pregnant, I needed an operation. However, the surgery to correct this condition was delicate and dangerous. The specialists had performed this surgery on only one woman, and she did not survive the operation. The doctor plainly stated that the woman died of blood loss on the operating table. That wasn't a risk that Dirk and I were willing to take.

The news was shocking. I was devastated. I desperately wanted to have children with my husband. I believed raising children was part of my responsibilities as a wife, and I had always wanted to become a mother.

I thought back to our church's Mother's Day service. The ushers gave flowers to the newest mom, the oldest mom, the one with the most children," and those with a mom in heaven, I didn't qualify for any of the categories. I felt incomplete, inadequate, and defective.

At a follow-up appointment, my doctor asked if we would consider the services of a surrogate. Dirk didn't have an opinion, but I was not ready to choose that answer. I thought back to Sarah, Abraham's wife, using her maid Hagar as a surrogate in Genesis 16:1-4 KJV. Sarah's choice had turned out badly, and I did not think to repeat that mistake was a good idea.

Instead, we decided to explore the possibility of adopting a child rather than having a birth child. Our relationship seemed to be going well. I complied with Dirk's requests, and he seemed more talkative and willing to do some of the hiking, picnics, and getting together with friends like we used to. Together, we completed the background checks, home study, and took the required seminars.

I love to create scrapbooks, and the idea of making one for a birth parent to use in making an adoption plan for her child was intimidating and exhilarating at the same time. I threw myself into it, determined to showcase what great parents we would be.

We talked a lot about the adoption process. Filling in all the paperwork took a long time. On a bright and sunny Sunday afternoon, while working through some of the most personal questions, the conversation turned to another woman I was counseling. Her husband had tried to push her down the stairs, and she didn't know what to do. Dirk became agitated and then angry. He seemed to misunderstand and thought that I was comparing him to the other man. "How could you believe that I would ever hurt you?" He came toward me, standing up straight, all 6'4" and 200 pounds of him. Looking up into his face, I saw pure indignation. Frightened by his loud, angry tirade, I ran to hide behind the coats in the downstairs coat closet.

Dirk yelled, "I'm going out for a while!" From the closet, I heard him slam the door and peel out of our driveway. Peeking out from the closet to glance out the window, I made sure he was gone. My hands were shaking as I sat on the couch. Not knowing what else to do, I called our assistant pastor's wife, Mrs. Smith. She came to sit and pray with me until Dirk came home. However, by 10:00 p.m., he had not yet returned. I assured her I would be fine, and she could go. "I'll call if I need something," I assured her.

Shortly after she left, Dirk came home. I expected him to have calmed down with the time passing, but he was even angrier. "I would never hurt you," he stated. "Why wouldn't you believe that?" He told me he had driven by our house but, seeing the car in the driveway, he refused to come inside. "I don't need the lectures," he snapped.

I apologized for making him angry. I honestly didn't mean to upset him. I explained that I wanted to share things that were important to me with my husband. Obviously, I should not have bothered him with that, he retorted. Why should he care? I took responsibility for the disagreement in order to smooth things out between us.

As time went on, Dirk was sent on another deployment; this time he was to be gone for three months--the entire summer. I had been moved from teaching first grade to sixth grade and was in my second year of teaching the same lessons. I made electronic presentations of the material and tried some newer lessons, but both the students and I were mostly disinterested. I realized that if

I was bored by the content I was supposed to teach, I could not make it very engaging for my students. I needed to do something different.

As I reflected on how to make my instruction more engaging, I came across a flyer for the Challenge Center for Space Science Education. Founded in 1986 by the families of the astronauts who had lost their lives in the Space Shuttle *Challenger* disaster, Challenger Center is a life-size simulator of a space mission. Housed at a school not far from where I taught, the center was offering a two-day seminar to teachers who would be willing to implement their program. I was approved to attend. I learned how to teach space science more effectively and was able to seamlessly integrate the Challenger Center activities with my school's sixth-grade science curriculum.

In the fall, I began teaching the Challenger program, "Mission to Rendezvous with a Comet." The students had to learn the science, technology, engineering, and math skills to make their mission successful. The kids were ecstatic!

Students would come to me first thing in the morning to see what I had planned for the science and math lessons. Our daily attendance was up, along with our test scores in every subject. The students were eager to come to school to learn so that they could participate in the Challenger mission. As I continued in the Challenger program, a class opened for perspective NASA Mission Space Educators. I received an invitation to join. The course helped me enhance my teaching skills and, as a bonus, involved preparing my grant application for the Eisenhower Foundation to become a NASA Mission Space Educator.

Besides having lots of fantastic projects for my students at the end of the class, I submitted my Eisenhower grant application. A few weeks later, I received a letter of acceptance into the NASA Mission Space Educator program. I had won the grant!

I was incredibly proud of myself, but that happy feeling didn't last long. Once again, I faced a decision. The Navy had reassigned Dirk to a different type of submarine out of Seattle, Washington. He would have a set schedule of deployment and be home more frequently. This deployment schedule would be better for our plans to have children. Plus, I would get to have Dirk around more often. Perhaps we could work on our relationship issues. It seemed like a good idea.

Still, I felt conflicted. I wanted to stay in Hawaii to continue teaching at the Christian school. I looked forward to my fellowship at the Hawaii Space Grant College to become a NASA mission space educator. I would have to give it all up if we moved to Washington State.

I read my Bible and prayed about it. I talked with Mrs. Smith, the assistant pastor's wife. I didn't want to, but I knew I needed to obey God by going with my husband. I claimed God's command that wives should follow the lead of their husbands just as we, as Christians, follow the lead of Jesus, the head of the church (Ephesians 5:22-33). In 1 Peter 3, wives are instructed to "respect and obey" their husbands. The passage continues with a comparison to Old Testament women who "obeyed" their husbands to the point of calling them "lord," (I Peter 3:1, 6 KJV).

I gave up my dream to move to Seattle.

11. BEGINNING OF THE END

"Husbands, love your wives, even as Christ also loved the church, and gave himself for it." – Ephesians 5:25 KJV

The move to Seattle was mostly smooth. We found a house to rent in a small town outside of the city. The house needed some repairs, so the owner rented it to us for a cheaper rate.

I quickly discovered I could not use the toaster and the microwave at the same time without flipping an electrical breaker. When I was baking something in the oven, I could not use the dishwasher, microwave, or toaster. And no other appliance could be on when I wanted to use the iron. So frustrating!

The house had an unusual number of unwanted guests: spiders. When I mentioned the problem to Dirk, he reminded me of an urban legend: "You unknowingly swallow an average of four live spiders in your sleep each year." When I had a hard time sleeping after hearing that, he laughed at me. While Dirk was checking into his new command, I scrubbed the house and swept out as many spiders and their accompanying webs as possible.

A cold snap and afternoon thaw led us to discover our rental had a leaky roof. When we mentioned the problem to a neighbor, he thought it had been leaking for years, and the owners hadn't gotten around to fixing it. He had stopped by to welcome us to the neighborhood with some of his freshly caught and freeze-dried salmon. I'd never seen a fish prepared like that before, but I thanked him, and he left.

Dirk and I began attending a small-town Baptist church. We soon came to love the pastor and his family. The church seemed an excellent fit for us. We became part of the congregation family, faithfully attending Sunday school and the worship service that followed, then the Sunday and Wednesday night prayer services. I taught the children's church sessions on Sunday mornings and Wednesday nights. I was thrilled to be able to serve God in a new place.

I found a job teaching at a small Christian school. I taught middle and high school English, middle school science, and geometry. Because Christian schools operate on a very tight budget, the principal assured me that I did not need teacher certification in any of those areas. I learned alongside the students.

Furthermore, our pastor joined me on the faculty as the Bible study teacher. The school hired several other teachers and their church's youth pastor who taught social studies. My pastor noticed that the young youth pastor seemed to flirt with the high school girls. I watched as he took the younger man aside and counseled him to "watch his testimony."

During this time, I met the Navy wives from Dirk's new command. We shared our experiences and became close friends. I volunteered for fundraisers and helped organize snacks for our meetings. As one of my first volunteer responsibilities, I picked up one hundred dozen Krispy Kreme donuts to deliver for a bake sale. We were raising money for a party for the children while their dads (our husbands) were out to sea. My car smelled wonderful—all sweet with the scent of fresh donuts.

I delighted in church fellowship dinners and meals with the pastor, elders, and their families. I became close friends with a group of ladies from the church. We soon became part of the exclusive inner circle. I suggested a summer vacation Bible school program that would last a whole month, and the church voted to support it. The kids came in the morning and stayed all day. Each day had a theme: Monday was craft day, Tuesday was sports day, Wednesday was water play day, Thursday was STEM day, and Friday was excursion day. STEM is an approach to learning and development that integrates science, technology, engineering, and math. The program was great fun.

One of the Thursdays Dirk came to the church for the rocket launch. He and I worked side by side with the ten children building and decorating their rockets. Then we took them to the big grassy church lawn. It warmed my heart to see Dirk smile and laugh with the children as they launched and then chased down their rockets as their tiny parachutes opened and drifted back to the ground. I thought it was a beautiful afternoon with Dirk and I together serving God and teaching the children.

The ladies of the church befriended me. We talked, traded recipes, shared memories, and studied what God's Word says about marriage. I thought that we had become close friends. However, during all this church and wives group involvement, Dirk and I continued to have difficulties in our relationship. I kept hoping our relationship would go back to how it had been before Dirk's illness on the submarine, but I wasn't getting anywhere.

I got the impression that Dirk didn't want to talk with me anymore. Every time I tried to share what was going on in my life, he would urge me to "get to the point" or "stop babbling." He only wanted to know about things that would directly affect him. He never shared anything that was happening at work or with his friends, despite my gentle questioning. He brushed me off if I tried to show interest in what he was doing.

It felt as if we were just jumping from one argument to another, with periods of uncomfortable silence in between. And, when we did fight, Dirk tormented me by yelling, "You're not a good Christian wife."

Dumbfounded and perplexed, I was in a state of mental shock. I had been a Christian School State Convention speaker. I taught all kinds of people in both adult ladies' groups and classrooms full of children but, somehow, I couldn't communicate with my husband. *Ouch.* No matter what I said, he found a way to be offended, even when I was complimenting him. My inability to make my husband happy nagged at me constantly. The distance between us was so frustrating.

We became fed up living in a house infested with spiders, electrical issues, and a leaky roof and decided to buy a home of our own. We hired a realtor who took us to look at several places, but we saw nothing that interested us. We were running out of options in our price range when our realtor showed us a condo in the small condominium community where she lived.

The two-bedroom, two-bath condo needed some paint and cleaning. Still, it had a fantastic view of the Olympic Mountains from the living room picture windows and some unique amenities, including a fireplace. We had planned for our child to have his/her bedroom and bathroom, so this condo was the right size. We jumped on it and were able to close and move in within a few months. I got right to work cleaning and painting. Dirk and one of our church friends, who happened to be a general contractor, ran network cables in the condo so that we could have faster internet service. Of course, this helped Dirk, who wanted to play his online computer games.

I wanted to find something Dirk and I could share in common. I began playing the massively multiplayer online role-playing game (MMORPG) that he played. Wondering how he could play for six to ten hours a day, I thought, *if he taught me how to play, we could play the game together.* I just wanted to have something in common with him again. This game felt like a stepping stone we could use to get back on the same page.

As I learned to play, I met people and chatted with them. A significant part of the game requires strategy and collaboration with other people to complete the missions. I met people from all over the United States, Mexico, Canada, and even a couple playing from the oilfields of the Canadian Arctic Circle. It takes efficient communication to direct twenty-five people to complete a mission. So, we would talk over headsets and microphones using a voice over internet protocol (VOIP) program, like a conference call for video gamers. These complicated tasks could take several hours to complete successfully and to divide the loot equitably.

Eventually, my character got to a higher level than Dirk's while he was out to sea. When he found out, he became upset and resentful. He accused me of slacking on my wifely duties to play the game and made disparaging remarks about how I spent my time. He made it clear how he thought I ought to be behaving, so

I tried doing exactly what Dirk said he wanted. I made sure to log off my computer when Dirk was due to be home. I made dinner every night and dressed up for him when he got back from work. I aspired to become his perfect wife, whatever I needed to do.

My relationship with Dirk fluctuated from good to terrible. First, he would tell me I was beautiful, smart, funny, and sexy, and then later, he would ignore me while he played his computer games and surfed pornography for hours. I felt as if I had to compete with his game. The only time he truly paid attention to me was when he wanted to be intimate. He continued to expect me to please him several times each day. I felt like I had whiplash from his continually shifting moods. This was not the marriage I had signed up for. I was miserable and didn't know what to do. How could I fix this? Surely God didn't intend for us to live so unhappily.

The next Sunday morning I felt God use the pastor's words to speak to my heart. I went forward to pray. Meeting the pastor at the altar, I shared my concerns and prayed with him. As we were leaving, he called Dirk into his office. After what seemed like an hour, Dirk finally came out. Outraged, he looked at me and quietly growled, "Get in the car! We're leaving now!" I was terrified! *What had our pastor done?*

As I buckled my seat belt, he warned, "Hold on." Dirk revved the engine and spun the tires sending the gravel from the parking lot flying as we sped out. He scolded me for telling the pastor just a small part of our ugly secrets. He savagely bellowed, "Our secrets are between you and me; they're no one else's business!"

He drove recklessly to frighten me, and his plan was working perfectly. Anxiously, I watched the speedometer climb over eighty miles per hour in a forty-five mile per hour zone. Dirk would get very close to the bumper of a car in front of us. Then he would slam on the brakes. Panicky, I held onto the grab handle above my head; my knuckles were white with the force of my grip. During the twenty-minute drive from the church to our condo, Dirk did that over and over again.

When we got home, I ran to the bedroom and locked the door. I collapsed on the bed in silent sobs. Dirk yelled through the door,

"That's what you get for embarrassing me!"

Terrified, I could barely speak, so in my mind, I prayed through my favorite verses. "I will lift up mine eyes unto the hills, from whence cometh my help? My help cometh from the LORD, which made heaven and earth" (Psalm 121:1-2 KJV). I vowed never, ever to talk with anyone about Dirk again. I hoped that God would find another way, but would He? Was this the way our marriage would be forever?

12. BABY ALLY

"For this child, I prayed; and the Lord hath given me my petition which I asked of him."
– I Samuel 1:27 KJV

In the meantime, we renewed our adoption process in Washington. I wondered if some of the tension in our marriage was due to the lack of a baby that we both desperately wanted. Sadly, our home study and background check that had been done in Hawaii did not count. Since we had to start over, we decided to adopt through a Christian adoption agency. Recreating our scrapbook for the prospective birth parents to get to know us was a labor of love. I hoped a biological mother would look through our album and choose us to parent her child.

In June, I received a call from the adoption agency that a biological mother wanted to interview us as prospective parents for her child. My mind raced. *How do we prepare for an interview to be a parent? What should I wear? What if she picks me?* And then, *What if she doesn't pick me?*

The agency was a two-hour drive from our condo. During the ride, Dirk and I talked about our answers to these questions and tried to think of several more. We were nervous. I enjoyed the peaceful conversation as we drove.

At the agency, we met the adoption counselors, biological mother, and her mother, Bio-gran. They were charming. We talked for almost an hour about the baby girl she was expecting and her hopes for her baby.

A week later, we received a call from the adoption agency. The biological mother wanted to interview us a second time, as she was deciding between us and another couple. All the nervousness returned regarding this interview. I considered being a parent one of the most important jobs ever. I felt as if my whole life had been leading up to this moment.

A few days after the meeting, our adoption counselor called with fantastic news. The biological mother had chosen us! We were going to be parents. Our daughter was to be born at the end of August. We had less than two months to prepare. Besides that, the birth mother wanted me to be in the delivery room when *our* daughter was born.

Since Dirk was one of the lowest Navy ranks, we didn't have much money. The pastor's wife and several of the church ladies recommended a local consignment shop to purchase baby furniture and all the necessities. We bought a cute, red metal crib and decided on a denim teddy bear theme. I decorated her nursery, and it quickly became my favorite room in our house. I wanted everything to be ready for our baby's arrival.

I read every book I could find about being a parent. I read about preparing homemade baby food, which baby formula is best, and compared book notes with two friends who were Navy wives. They were also expecting while I was waiting for our daughter to be born. One friend gave birth to a girl, and the other had twins, one boy, and one girl.

My Navy wife friends and I happily planned baby "playdates" while our husbands were on deployment. We continued reading and studying parenting books. As part of all our planning, we made baby announcements to send out the minute our babies were born. Since I considered Ally a gift, God's answer to my prayers, my card included this verse, "For this child I prayed, and the LORD hath given me my petition which I asked of him," (I Samuel 1:27 KJV).

One afternoon the adoption counselor called to say the birth mother was in labor and to come to the hospital as soon as possible. When we arrived all excited and ready, we discovered she was having false labor contractions. We returned disappointed to our condo. When a second call came, we rushed to the hospital only to be disappointed and return home once again.

I was somewhat skeptical when the phone rang a third time. We heard the same message again: the birth mother was in labor, and our baby was coming soon. Grabbing our overnight bags and baby items, we flew out the door. The hospital was over an hour's drive, including a short ferry ride.

Once at the hospital, we were escorted to a room down the hall from our birth mother's room. A hospital bracelet identified me as a "birth mother's baby" parent. My parents had also come for the birth of our baby girl.

From another room, we waited for the birth mother to allow us to see her. In her room, we renewed our acquaintance, and I introduced my parents as the adoptive grandparents. The birth mother was thrilled that her baby would have such a supportive extended family.

The birth mother had been in labor for quite a while. I held her hand waiting for our baby's arrival as our mothers bonded over stories of when she and I were little girls. Her spirits lightened as we talked and shared stories.

At exactly 10:00 a.m., baby Ally made her appearance. I was holding the birth mother's hand, and our moms were holding hands around her. Dirk had decided to wait outside with my dad.

Shortly after her birth, it became evident that Ally was in distress. The doctors and nurses placed her on the birth mother's chest for what seemed like thirty seconds. Ally was too warm, and her skin was not the right color. The team then put her on a table with a warming lamp as they checked her over.

She was running a dangerously high fever at 103.7° from what the doctors eventually diagnosed as a massive infection. The medical team inserted an IV in her foot and covered her tiny body with electrical devices. We stood in silent shock as she was taken to the Neonatal Intensive Care Unit (NICU).

Stricken, the birth mother sobbed, "I knew she was ready to come last week; why did they send me home?" She was so exhausted, and I hugged her. In truth, I was also exhausted.

With nothing else to do, we returned to our assigned space to wait. After a couple of restless hours, we were allowed back into the biological mother's room to see her and Ally. We took a few pictures. Ally's birthmother shared that she had chosen a middle name to honor her grandfather. She asked us if we would keep that name to help Ally remember how much her birth family had loved her.

"Of course," I agreed, wiping tears from my eyes.

The biological mother passed Ally to her mother, who then gave her to my family members—Dirk, my mom, my dad, and, lastly, to me. I was still overwhelmed at the thought that Ally's birth mother would give me this precious gift. Ally would be going home with me in a day or two.

I didn't hear Dirk as he whispered to my mom that I held Ally last because I was probably not ready for the responsibility of a baby. She told me later about his whispers, which planted doubts about my being able to be a good parent because I was too emotional.

In Washington, biological parents who have previously signed adoption papers for their babies are given forty-eight hours as a parental termination waiting period. During this time, the biological mother and I both received training in how to provide Ally with primary infant care, diapering, bathing, and CPR. The nurses also trained Dirk and my parents.

Ally had a monitor on her umbilical cord that would set off an alarm if she left the hospital maternity ward. Ally's ankle identification bracelet matched her birth mother's and my bracelets. Dirk and I had our picture taken for the nurses to identify us as we came to visit the NICU. My parents also made friends with the nursing staff.

The biological mother and I took turns feeding Ally. Seeing her attached to all the medical monitors was heart-wrenching. We had to be careful not to bump her leg with the IV and to hold her just right to arrange all the tubes comfortably.

Ally already had strong opinions of what she wanted—even in the NICU. When the nurses straightened her blankets, she made a sound like a growl. At feeding time, she was the loudest baby, by far! I thought this was good news—it showed that she was a fighter!

Because of her medical issues when she was born, the neonatal pediatricians tested Ally for spinal meningitis and several other chronic debilitating diseases. She failed the hearing test and was labeled "hard of hearing." The prognosis, though, was encouraging. The doctors told us not to worry—that she would "grow out of it in a month or two." All the tests eventually came back negative.

The day after Ally was born, Dirk received a call saying he needed to go back to work. I was overwhelmed with all the emotions and medical tests. The "what-ifs" haunted me. *How can the Navy be so heartless as to take Dirk when we are still at the hospital with a newborn in the NICU?* I called the command, speaking to the Chief of the Boat, whose wife was my friend. He assured me that Dirk was not considered essential and could stay with me. I was relieved by his assurances; however, Dirk was unsure. He seemed uncomfortable at the hospital with all the uncertainties.

Staying at the hospital all this time, we met with our adoption counselor and frequently stopped in to see Ally's biological mother. The forty-eight-hour waiting period before the court would execute the birth mother's adoption plan to terminate her parental rights seemed to take forever. As Ally had made her appearance on a Thursday, the forty-eight-hour waiting period meant our adoption attorney could not present our paperwork to the court until Monday, more than the required forty-eight hours.

My parents, Dirk, and I prayed. I cried. We talked with the biological mother's adoption counselor and our counselor, continuing to spend as much time with Ally as we could. The biological mother kept Ally in her room as much as possible and all night for a final goodbye.

Before Ally was born, we had planned to have the birth grandmother's Lutheran church minister give Ally her Christian name, baptize her, and officiate her adoption in the eyes of God and the church. My parents would be present, along with the biological grandmother and our adoption counselors. I was so relieved when it was finally time for the ceremony.

As we entered the birth mother's hospital room for the service, she and her mother were already crying as they held Ally, who was still attached to all of the monitoring machines. The Lutheran minister introduced himself and explained he had brought holy water to the hospital and a certificate of baptism for Ally. I had no idea this ceremony would be so gut-wrenching.

The minister asked the biological mother to hold Ally while he prayed to bless her, announced her Christian name, and anointed her with holy water. He then requested Ally's biological mother to give the baby to me. When she passed Ally to me, we both cried.

The minister said a few words about the importance of rearing Ally to be a good Christian young lady. He continued with his devotional, saying her adoption was symbolic of our adoption into God's family. Every eye in the room was full of tears. The nurse who came to make sure Ally's cords, cables, and machines were all functioning well gave us a box of tissues from the cabinet, first taking a tissue for herself. She was moved to tears, too.

We exchanged gifts. Ally's birth mother gave me her baby. In a feeble attempt to express my gratitude, I made her a picture album in which to place pictures of Ally that I would send as she grew up. On the flyleaf, I had put an adoption poem: *A child with two mothers--one who carried the baby in her body and the other who held the baby in her heart.*

Our mothers exchanged hugs. The minister prayed to bless both families and especially Ally. I kept hugging her birth mother as she continued to sob.

"Thank you. Thank you! I'll never be able to thank you enough," I whispered.

We left the room and headed back to the NICU with the teary-eyed nurse helping us with all the mobile medical equipment still attached to Ally. We tearfully took her back to the NICU.

We never saw our baby's biological mother leave the hospital.

Ally spent a total of seven days in the NICU enduring tests and having all the equipment attached to her. She loved sitting in the baby swing, which the nurses adjusted to accommodate all her cords and cables. She also loved being cuddled in the rocking chair.

Dirk and I were thrilled when the doctors finally decided Ally could go home. The nurses inspected the car seat for the proper installation. They helped us ensure Ally was buckled correctly for the ride home. The hospital had given us handmade quilts for her in the NICU, so we snuggled them around her to keep her warm.

I was so excited to get Ally home, but, as with any newborn, she did not sleep very long. She would scream when we tried to bathe her and seemed not to like things lightly touching her body. When the social worker visited, she reminded me that Ally had been exposed to illicit drugs when her birth mother was expecting her. Even though her biological mother had reported using drugs four times. Still, the social worker stated that, in her experience, the reality was usually at least four times more.

Dirk went back to work, leaving me with Ally and my parents during the day. I tried to rest when Ally did, but I could hardly believe I had a baby girl. She was beautiful. I loved to watch her sleep peacefully in her swing or crib, but at night Dirk watched Ally while I slept. He said that he liked to stay up late anyway.

My mom told me later that Dirk expressed concern that I was not "bonding" with Ally. He shared that his worries that I was not able to take care of her "like a good mom." Looking back now, I understand that Dirk was trying to manipulate my mother into doubting that I was a good parent. If he could convince my mother that I was a bad parent, he would continue to be in control of every aspect of my life.

The time came again for Dirk to go on deployment. I was unsure how I was going to handle being all alone with a newborn baby. My parents had flown home; Dirk left. What would I do?

In answer to a prayer I hadn't prayed yet, the first night he was gone, Ally slept through the night. She continued to sleep through the night during Dirk's full six-month deployment! God allowed me to get the sleep I needed to be Ally's mom.

13. REALIZATION

"The eyes of the Lord are in every place, beholding the evil and the good."
— Proverbs 15:3 KJV

Dirk said we should sell our condominium overlooking the Olympic Mountains to move into Navy housing. He thought it would save us some money and give us more space. I had quit my teaching job the summer before Ally was born and planned to be a stay-at-home mom until she was old enough to go to school. Besides, we would be closer to his job and not have any upkeep on our place. The condo didn't have enough space for us with all of Ally's baby furniture and Dirk's computer equipment.

We moved into a larger apartment on the Navy base. Besides having two bedrooms and two bathrooms, it also had a dedicated laundry and storage room, living room, kitchen with a breakfast nook, and a dining room. Reasoning that we could eat in the kitchen, Dirk turned the dining room into his office space.

The Navy owned the properties but leased them to a private management company. Dirk paid our rent by signing his housing allowance as a direct deposit to them, and the money covered all our home expenses except our internet, television, and phones.

The apartment was on the second floor, but our first-floor neighbors were cordial and quiet. They seemed to be rarely home. I made them homemade bread and strawberry jam from strawberries Dirk and I had picked. Along with the goodies, I added an invitation to church.

One afternoon while Ally was napping, I was playing the online computer game when a virtual friend, Tim, made an unsought observation. "I think you're in an abusive relationship. Your husband treats you like a maid with benefits."

"What?! Why would you say such a thing?"

Dirk loved me; I knew it. He told me so all the time. The thought that my husband would use me was unimaginable.

"I just need to try harder," I responded.

I continued to play online, talking on the internet with the people I had met in the game. I was isolated from the people around me, but while playing the game I felt like I had friends. At least I had something in common with the other players. I could talk with them on those days when I couldn't have a complete conversation with my husband without making him upset or telling me that I talk too much about things that he didn't want to hear.

Dirk became paranoid. He accused me of having a "virtual affair" because one person I played with frequently, Tim, would use the game communication system to check on me every day. As an Iraqi war army veteran, Tim was brave enough to confront me with the truth: my husband was abusive. Dirk was especially jealous of Tim because he reminded me often that my husband was using me. Dirk grew to hate Tim.

In return for his helping me, Dirk cyber-stalked him. He researched Tim on the internet, then he called his house to threaten him and even logged into our computer game in an attempt to bully and intimidate him, so he wouldn't encourage me to get help.

Tim announced my husband was abusive, and he maintained his conclusion. I had never, ever even considered the possibility. No one else dared to say anything as Tim had declared. Was Dirk abusing me? Didn't he love me? How could a Christian marriage be abusive? Was I one of those women in the domestic violence posters who needed to call a special phone number because they were being hurt? Didn't that only happen to uneducated and non-Christian people?

Justified by his obsession with my "virtual affair," Dirk began a routine of checking my computer and my phone history without my permission and at his whim. Dirk thoroughly examined all the documents on my computer, making sure I wasn't going to embarrass him again as I had done at the church in front of the pastor.

Answering our apartment door was out of the question. Even responding to our house telephone was not allowed. If I didn't give him my phone, he would look at our bill online to see who I was calling. He yelled at me about my "virtual affair" on a continuous basis. He would not tolerate my leaving the house unless he knew where I was going, who I was going to see, and when I would return. Dirk's restrictions were huge red flags of abuse that I had missed. He was controlling the people I was allowed to see and hang out with, where I went, and even when I could go out.

Another afternoon during Ally's naptime, I was updating pictures on Ally's baby website to share with both her biological family and adoptive family. But Dirk decided I needed to service him sexually--right at that moment. When I dared to tell him, "Not now," he tapped his penis on my shoulder! I couldn't believe his actions. *Why on earth would he do that?* As I tried to push him away, he pulled back my rolling computer chair and began tickling me.

Reluctantly, I realized where this was going, and I gave in. I had said, "No, I don't want to now," but I knew it was futile. Dirk would overpower me, and I would have more bruises for resisting. He wrestled me to the carpeted office floor and repeated the all-too-familiar words, "You'll like it when I'm done with you." I tried to think about anything else until he was done. I got up from the floor, tried to straighten my wrinkled clothes, and walked off to the bathroom to clean myself up.

I tried to go along with Dirk's restrictions to keep him from being upset with me. I quickly learned not to call anyone, not even the other Navy wives, when Dirk was home; I knew that would anger him. I made all my calls while he was at work and sometimes from the parking lot at the grocery store or shopping mall. I felt isolated, but what could I do?

14. DEPLOYMENT

*"For he shall give his angels charge over thee, to keep thee in all thy
ways." - Psalm 91:11 KJV*

Dirk's submarine was on a schedule: three months at sea, then
three months at home. It was time for his deployment. I emailed
Dirk, but the boat's location and operational status limited all
communications. Messages were censored and not delivered if the
commanding officer thought it would be disruptive to their
mission--unless it was an emergency. I didn't email Dirk. I was
relieved that he was gone. There was so much less stress when he
was away. I didn't have to walk on egg shells worrying what was
going to make him upset at me at any moment. But I was also
conflicted. I felt a bit guilty for not missing him more. One of my
Navy wife friends, Carlee, commented that I seemed like a
different person, happier somehow. But why did I feel guilty?
Were our communication problems my fault?

While he was at sea, Ally and I went on the playdates that I had
planned with my friends before our babies were born. Our first
visit was to Kelly, who had just given birth to twins. Two of every
piece of baby furniture, including swings, sat in her living room.
Kelly was exhausted from caring for her babies and craved adult
company. Ally and I arrived at the house, and Kelly put one baby
in a swing and the other in a playpen. She invited me to put Ally
in the now-empty swing. As I was finishing buckling the safety
belts, her dog came over to check out the new baby. Her dog,

named D-O-G, was a female boxer and was very protective of the babies. She sniffed Ally and laid down at the foot of the swing. Kelly said that D-O-G had accepted Ally as one of her babies to guard. It was sweet.

I loved spending time with Kelly and her babies while our husbands were out to sea. We enjoyed laughing and sharing new mom stories until it was naptime or bedtime. Those routines were firm boundaries. Besides, we needed the rest, too.

Our apartment was just around the corner from my friend Carlee. I was thrilled to be able to hang out with her at a moment's notice. We could meet for playdates at the small playground that was within walking distance of both of our homes. Our kids got along so well. Being able to spend time with a close friend when our husbands were out to sea was great. Dirk and Carlee's husband served on the same submarine.

On Ally's first birthday, Carlee and her kids celebrated with us. First, we met for a birthday lunch at McDonald's. Ally flashed a massive smile as I put French fries from her Happy Meal on the placemat of her high chair. She picked up one in each hand and alternated taking a bite from each. The sight was darling.

Carlee's kids ate Happy Meals, too. Her kids were aged two and three and loved the park. After lunch, we walked the kids to the park between our houses to eat birthday cupcakes and play. There were two swings for three children, but the kids were kind to each other and took turns. We were proud of their excellent behavior toward each other. Carlee's kids took turns gliding down the slide, but Ally didn't want to leave the swing. She only agreed after we presented her birthday cupcakes. I held Ally in one arm and, with my other hand, held the cupcake out to her, expecting her to take it from me. Instead of taking it, she lowered her head and took a bite resulting in white frosting and rainbow sprinkles spread out across her chin. Her brown eyes sparkled as she signed, "more, more, more." I had read that babies can use American Sign Language before they learn to speak, and Ally had learned quite a few words such as hungry, thirsty, more, no, yes, please, and thank you. "No" was becoming her favorite word to sign.

She and Carlee's kids sat at the picnic table to eat their

cupcakes. I had put Ally down as I realized she wasn't going to take the cupcake if I was holding it. When they finished eating all the frosting, and very little of the cake-part, Ally signed "all done." Carlee and I used wet wipes to clean the kids. We swept up the cupcake crumbs from the picnic table and took the kids to our separate homes for naptime. It had been a full day for three little ones.

15. COUNSELING

"Hear counsel, and receive instruction, that thou mayest be wise in thy latter end." – Proverbs 19:20 KJV

Carlee and I talked through our days about husbands and kids as the children played together. She had noticed the difference between how I acted and looked when Dirk was home and when he was out to sea. We had talked about his controlling behavior with answering the door, using the phone, and telling him when, where, and with whom I was going out. We talked a little about our sex lives, as Navy wives do, but I didn't share anything too shocking. I had been punished for that before.

As a result of our daily talks, Carlee suggested I see a Navy family counselor. The counselors were fantastic and had helped her quite a bit. She was sure they could also help me.

Since Dirk had returned from deployment, I spoke with him about the idea of getting some counseling; perhaps they could help us communicate better. I wanted our marriage to be as happy as I remembered it at the beginning. He agreed but, in his opinion, he wasn't the one who needed any counseling. It was all my fault. To Dirk, I was a mess who needed all the help I could get. He approved, saying, "Go, figure out what's wrong with you." He didn't need a counselor; he was fine the way he was.

With Dirk's approval and Carlee's insistence, I completed what seemed like a mountain of paperwork and was finally able to make an appointment with the Navy Family Services Center. Every military base has a safe place whose mission is to address abuse, neglect, and problematic sexual behavior in children and young people. I had access because Dirk was in the Navy, and I knew of the resources by working with our Navy Wives' Group. God used these people to help save my life.

Once I reserved the appointment, Dirk's constant taunts of "You're so angry all the time; You're not a good Christian wife; You don't meet all *my* needs," only increased. Of course, he insisted that he did not need any counseling; I was the one in desperate need. Nothing was wrong with him.

Something had to change; Dirk seemed to be angry at me all the time. We needed help. I knew it. I didn't grasp how badly I needed help; our marriage had its share of problems, but I had no idea it was abusive. I was in denial. My friends noticed the signs that Dirk was abusing me before I did. I couldn't see it. Or maybe I just couldn't admit it to myself. I thought I could be a better wife or work harder to improve my marriage.

My mind came up with endless excuses:

Dirk loves me. He can't possibly be an abuser.

I must not be a good enough Christian wife if my husband does these things.

I just need to pray more and work to change myself.

I thought that if I became Dirk's perfect wife, our marriage would miraculously be perfect. After all, God gave us the perfect child we desired.

At one of my first sessions, my counselor explained that domestic violence is all about the power and control of the abuser. The abuser needs to be in control of every situation. As an example, she reminded me that when I shared my concerns with our pastor, Dirk was no longer in control, so he used the car ride to intimidate me.

With her help, I identified many of the ways Dirk had manipulated me from the power and control wheel of abuse. Besides intimidation, Dirk had used isolation when I was not allowed out of the house without his permission, and not allowed to answer the phone or door. He blamed me for all his troubles. He said he loved me then humiliated me with physical and sexual abuse, coercion, and threats.

My counselor and I mulled over my communication issues, such as the ones between Dirk and me, between my students and me, and as a mentor and conference speaker. I seemed to be able to communicate with all these people, both individually and in groups, but not with my husband. What was *my* problem?

During another session, we discussed Dirk's and my sex life. Her first question caught me off guard. "How often do you have sex?" She followed up this question with, "How often do you think is normal or average?" I was taken aback by her forwardness. I never discussed this with anyone; talking about sex was taboo.

I recited the verse that our pastor had used, and Dirk had quoted to me numerous times: "Marriage is honorable in all, and the bed undefiled…" (Hebrews 13:4 KJV). I did not want to believe that the pastor interpreted the verse the same way that Dirk did. He always badgered me into submitting to his sexual perversions with the last half of the verse, "the bed undefiled." He twisted the meaning so that he could do anything to me in our bed, and I had to submit—no matter what. Cautiously, I spoke of Dirk's insatiable sex drive; he wanted to have sex with me five or six times a day. His disturbing demands caused me severe anxiety and distress.

In sessions with my counselor, I reflected on Dirk's and my conversations. Her patient guidance led me to the realization that I am allowed personal space—even from my husband. Dirk had no right to molest me all the time. My counselor suggested that I set sexual limits. In the safety of her office, she and I practiced what I would say and what Dirk's response would be.

When I got home, I began telling Dirk, "No." I even tried, "Not now." However, the next time Dirk made advances, he ignored my "No." He proclaimed that I was his to touch when and wherever he wanted. If I were a good Christian wife, I would obey him. Nevertheless, I quickly learned that my saying "No" or even "Not now" caused Dirk to become much angrier. He grabbed me, began tickling me, and wrestled me to the floor. He pinned me to the floor with his body weight and repeated the statement I had heard frequently: "You'll like it when I'm inside of you."

I had tried to fight him off, even leaving bruises on his arms. However, he was 6'2" and almost 200 pounds. I was nearly a foot shorter and 50 pounds smaller. I could not stop him from forcing himself on me. He relished having power over me. Dirk's idea of intimacy did not match what I had understood the act of marriage to be in our premarital counseling sessions. "I am my beloved's, and his desire is toward me," (Song of Solomon 7:10 KJV). Dirk forced himself on me at his every whim sneering, "You will fulfill my every fantasy."

As I endured his continuous molestations, I would try to focus on anything other than what he was doing to my body. I became detached; my mind disconnected from my body as a survival mechanism. While Dirk was raping me, my brain made "to-do" lists consisting of household chores such as buying groceries, washing clothes, planning meals, and cleaning the house.

I moaned and pretended to go along with him, hoping beyond hope that he would finish faster. I hoped and prayed I didn't have to meet his needs again anytime soon. I was not allowed to leave the bed in the morning without having sex with Dirk or at least giving him a "hand job" until he was satisfied. When he was done with me, I could start my day.

My counselor listened compassionately to my confessions. I felt safe confessing Dirk's and my secrets to her. She was bound by health care privacy laws, so I trusted her. After discussing Dirk's thorough inspection of my computer documents, she showed me an infographic about the cycle of domestic violence similar to the one below. I still didn't want to admit that Dirk was abusive, but when I read the parts of the cycle, I saw the stages of my life for the past few months.

In yet another intense counseling session, I shared how Dirk

81

was threatening to make his internal rage external. I told her how he paused his computer game and turned toward me as we played on our separate computers together in the office. I had no idea what he would say or do. My mind raced with, "What did I do?" "Why is he angry at me?" "How can I make whatever he is upset about be okay?"

He seemed sad, rather than angry this time, sharing about a shipmate who told the submarine's captain that he was a dragon inside, and his dragon was going to flame everyone for being mean to him. Dirk said he identified with this guy; he, too, was tired of people being mean to him. "I don't have a dragon inside, but I want to take the rage that he was feeling inside and direct it outside." He stated this flatly, giving me no reason to think he was joking. Truthfully, I wondered if I were on the list of people who he considered mean to him. Would he kill me?

Alarmed, my counselor began firing questions at me. "Are you telling me that Dirk intends to harm himself or others? Are you sure that you want to tell me that Dirk is threatening to harm himself or others? Does he have access to guns or weapons? Do you understand the consequences of what you're telling me?"

As a conscientious Christian woman, a Navy wife mentor, and a professional educator, I knew that Dirk and I needed help. I understood saying those words would require my counselor to notify Dirk's commanding officer. In answer to an unspoken prayer, God gave me the courage to do the right thing. I told her I understood the significance of what I had told her.

Dirk had frequently talked about death and made comments such as, "The world would be a better place without me in it." I told her how he had threatened to move to Southeast Asia and change his name so I would not be able to find him. He continually badgered me, saying, "You will become a single parent and have to take care of Ally all by yourself."

I recalled a rare, brave moment when I countered, "You go out to sea almost nine months a year anyway. What difference will it make?" I instantly regretted that response. His menacing scowl betrayed his intentions, and I knew I was in trouble. Immediately enraged, Dirk ordered, "Go to the bedroom!" Ally was napping, and normally I didn't dare disobey; I was petrified. When I didn't do as he asked, sometimes he pouted and refused to speak to me. Other times he raged at me, or I ended up with bruises. What could I do? Besides, isn't a Christian wife supposed to love, cherish, and to obey her husband? "Wives submit to your own husbands," (Ephesians 5:22 KJV) is the command. To continue to obey God, wasn't I required to comply?

I paid dearly for my defiant remarks. Dirk tied me to the bed; he tied the scarves used to restrain me so tightly that they left marks which later became bruises on both my wrists and ankles. When he finished using me, he left me naked, bound there, to gloat over my humiliation. Daring to look up at his face, I saw his perverse smile, as if he were proud of his conquest. Every part of my body felt battered by his cruel treatment. I closed my eyes for what seemed like an hour, hoping he could not see my tears. How could someone who said he loves me treat me with such disrespect and cruelty? After a few minutes, Dirk finished humiliating me, so he untied me. I quickly grabbed clean clothes, went to the bathroom and locked the door. I took a hot shower, but nothing could wash off the humiliation.

My counselor, required by law to report any suspicion of domestic violence or threats of bodily harm, disclosed Dirk's behavior to his commanding officer. Because of these reports, his command required Dirk to undergo psychiatric evaluations, attend sessions with counselors, and to take several different medications. He fumed; it was all my fault. His security clearance withdrawn, he could not go on the three-month deployment with his submarine as scheduled. He was ordered to attend anger management class for a week and was transferred to a temporary shore command after being declared unfit for duty on his submarine. Being at home more often with Ally and me, Dirk took every opportunity to condemn me. He couldn't see that it was his hurtful, abusive actions that had caused his current situation. Instead, it was all my fault; I did this to him.

The Navy made Dirk take leave (vacation) for ten days due to all his medical appointments and anger management classes. Arriving home from class, he recapped the day's lesson as if I were his student. He seethed that *I* should be going to class; I was the angry one, not him. "It's all your fault," he screamed. I endured his taking every opportunity to point out my shortcomings as often as possible.

I never knew what was going to make him angry. One evening a couple we knew from church came to visit us, and Dirk allowed me to answer the door. I invited them to go and sit in the living room and brought everyone coffee and a plate of cookies. As they talked with us about the weather and upcoming church events, they asked if I could call someone else. I replied that I probably could not call anyone else. Continuing the conversation, I mentioned that I was not allowed to use the phone or answer the door without my husband's permission. I wondered what they would say. Would she whisper to me, asking if I needed help as she hugged me on the way out of our home? Would someone notice the odd behavior between Dirk and me? I almost dared to hope, but no. They discounted my offhand comment by saying, "That's probably for the best. The world's not safe for anyone anymore." I would receive no help from them.

One night when I answered my cell phone without Dirk's permission, he grabbed it out of my hand and threw it against the wall as Ally toddled by. The phone shattered just inches above her head. "That will teach you," he snapped.

I was outraged, but I held back tears. "I can't believe you did that! You almost hit Ally." I did not allow myself to show my horror; I already knew the consequences of expressing my feelings. The next day Dirk apologized and took me to purchase a new phone, so I could call a doctor if Ally happened to need one.

This incident was a perfect example of the cycle of abuse. Tensions built as Dirk was monitoring my phone use. He exploded, grabbed my phone and hurled it against the wall just over Ally's head as she toddled by, and then the reconciliation as Dirk took me to purchase a new phone so I could call Ally's doctor.

We had calm for a while until the tensions began building again. I was told Dirk went to my counselor's office and took cell phone pictures of the layout. My counselor was frightened and called the military police who ordered him to stay away from her office. Dirk agreed reluctantly because he did not want to go to a Navy jail.

One evening my friend Jen called to invite Dirk and me to dinner. I was excited to be getting out of the house, and Dirk seemed to think we would have a good time. He and Jen's husband were friends who had served on the same boat. As she invited me, Jen asked if she could say something. "Is it safe to talk?" I thought it was a strange question, but she continued, "I asked Dirk just now if he still loved you and after he hesitated, he said, 'no!'"

I couldn't believe what I had heard. "Excuse me? Why would you ask that?"

Jen continued, "I want you to know your situation. We are concerned."

I assured her that Dirk did love me; he made me recite it to him all the time: "I'm smart; I'm funny; I'm sexy; I'm loved." He must have misunderstood your question, I defended. I knew Dirk loved me; he was having some medical and mental health problems, that's all. Our marriage vows before God were "in sickness and in health." I trusted that God would make everything better. I knew He could fix our relationship to be healthier than ever.

On my next weekly visit, I told my counselor that I felt unsafe, but I didn't think Dirk would hurt Ally or me. The counselor suggested that I make a safety plan. She said that one could never know when verbal abuse could become physical, and I should prepare. She insisted that I was in danger. Although I naively dismissed my counselor, I did make a safety plan with her just in case. So, if things did get out of control, I would know what to do. I knew there would be people who would help.

In my safety plan, I decided upon a person I would call when things went badly. I thought that my friend Rhonda, the command ombudsman, (Navy wife command liaison), was the right choice. She had the connections and training to deal with a potentially explosive situation, not that I believed that I would ever need it, of course.

My counselor emphasized the idea that the plan could only work if I had my cell phone within reach at all times. She also suggested that I pack a "go-bag" with a change of clothes, money, car keys, and copies of essential documents to keep in my car or close to the door, in case I could not go back to my home safely.

I kept my essential papers in a large manila envelope hidden in a dark backpack in the trunk of my car. I never expected that I would need them, but I would discover that I did! I picked the most critical papers from the list my counselor gave me. I included copies of my military identification and driver's license. I put the checkbook, medical insurance cards, marriage certificate, birth certificates, passport, social security cards, and our rental agreement in the envelope, too.

Dirk was angry and suspicious because of what I shared with my counselor. When he questioned me about that particular appointment my answers infuriated him. How could I think that he would say such a thing? He would never hurt anyone. Once again, it was all my fault. He considered talking to my counselor about him as a betrayal. He stalked off. Since I was fearful, I called my counselor, who made an immediate appointment for me, resulting in the MPs serving Dirk with a restraining order. The order required that Dirk sleep in the barracks and stay away from our apartment. He was not to contact Ally or me for five days.

However, he told his command that he needed clothes and shoes. They had the MPs ask me to leave the house for a couple of hours. The MPs suggested I go to a friend's house so Dirk could pick up some of his belongings. Dirk may have picked up his supplies, but he also left behind a tower of Reese's Peanut Butter cups, my favorite candy, on my desk alongside a tower of baby food for Ally. His peace offering looked like a shrine. The entire scene was disturbing.

Dirk spent his five days in the barracks and was allowed to come home. I made his favorite dinner, bringing his plate to the computer, where he planned to sit for hours. His restraining order was my fault, but at least I didn't have bruises this time. He said he didn't mean to scare me. I must have misunderstood him. He would never hurt me on purpose; I just bruised easily. Again, he insisted it was all my fault.

Another week passed with an uneasy truce; I didn't know

where or when the next explosion would come, only that it would happen eventually. My life had been in that cycle over the last few months.

The day came for my next weekly meeting with my counselor. Of course, Dirk allowed me to go. I needed the help, in his opinion. As we talked, I expressed my fear of Dirk's explosions and his command permitting him to go back into our house whenever he asked.

As I talked through these situations with my counselor, she reminded me that domestic violence runs in a cycle. The cycle begins with tension, and then there is an explosion after which comes reconciliation and calm until the next pressure builds, and the cycle continues until the victim leaves. According to National Domestic Violence statistics, it takes between seven and twelve times of being severely abused before a victim escapes. I did not want to be one of those statistics.

With the help of my counselor, I was beginning to understand that when I felt as if I had to "walk on eggshells," not knowing what would make Dirk mad the next time, I was entering the tension building stage. I tried to do as he asked, but I was not always successful. I never understood what caused Dirk to explode. Sometimes I would disturb him by speaking to him while he was playing his computer game or watching television. Other times, I could talk to him without causing an explosion. Then on a different day, I would make a meal of which he did not approve, and he would explode again.

One time I did not remember to purchase soda at the grocery store, and we ran out. Dirk shrieked at me for not keeping track of how much soda was in our house. I didn't drink it, but I should have purchased more from the grocery store. He refused to speak to me for the rest of the day. I couldn't go to the grocery store that day due to Ally's doctor appointments, so I promised Dirk that I would go first thing in the morning. I was continually trying to appease him. I had to shift and adjust my behavior to keep him from exploding. When he repeatedly remarked that I "babble" and "mumble" about things that no one wants to know, I tried to condense my conversations. I attempted to make his favorite foods, although I found it very difficult to meet his changing demands.

I kept Ally away from Dirk. I tried to keep her quiet and only brought her to him when he wanted to see her or play with her. It seemed that Dirk considered Ally as a toy to be taken down from the shelf and played with until he tired of her. At other times he didn't want to hear or see her. He would instruct me to put on a video so she wouldn't disturb us. What he meant was that I should put on a video so she wouldn't see him abusing me. After each explosion, Dirk would purchase candy or flowers for me and Ally's favorite baby food or a small toy to make amends. He would wait until I left the house with Ally and then stack them in a pyramid shape on my desk. Dirk never apologized. I understood that he would never hurt me unless I made him angry. It was just hard to tell what would trigger that anger.

Dirk told me at the beginning of our dating relationship that his father had abused both Dirk and his mother. He said that he didn't know how to be a good man except to trust God and do everything the opposite of his father. I was so happy to hear it. But words do not always translate into actions. The messages I was getting from Dirk now were along the lines of, "I understand why my father threw my mother over a fence and into a pool. She made him so angry." I couldn't believe what I was hearing. How could a Christian man think that hurting someone, his mother especially, was appropriate? Was this the same man I had married? What was happening in my life? I had always tried to be good. I followed all the rules from the Bible as my Christian duty. Why was my life falling apart? Wouldn't God help me?

At the next weekly meeting with my counselor, I expressed my fear of Dirk's explosions and his command permitting him to go back into our home whenever he asked. My counselor told me to find some friends to stay with for a few days, and they would talk with Dirk. His commanding officer ordered him to meet with a counselor to help calm the situation and work on our differences. So, with our apartment being unsafe, I fled. The head elder of my church and his wife allowed me to stay in their home with them. I thought I knew them well. Their son was in my English class at the Christian school; they had hosted Ally's baby shower, and Joyce and I went shopping together at the mall. She made gorgeous quilts; her home looked as if it came from Better Homes and Gardens Magazine. She was teaching me her favorite gourmet cooking techniques. I considered Joyce, to be my Christian wife mentor.

Joyce and Mark agreed to let Ally and me stay with them on the condition that I meet with our pastor. I was happy to have him come to read the Bible and pray with me. Prayer is always the answer, right? We sat at the kitchen table as the pastor opened his Bible to Psalm 51. "Have mercy on me, O God, according to your unfailing love; according to your great compassion blot out my transgressions. Wash away all my iniquity and cleanse me from my sin. For I know my transgressions and my sin is always before me," (Psalm 51:1-3 KJV).

"Confess your sin," the pastor pressed. He advised me to discuss it with him and the elder and his wife. In my heart, I wondered why they needed to know. I had always confessed my sins directly to God, "who is faithful and just to forgive us our sins and to cleanse us from all unrighteousness," (I John 1:9 KJV). I had never taken into account that I should confess to other people.

Head bowed in shame, I gazed up into Mark's and Joyce's faces. I recalled them saying I needed to pray with the pastor as a condition of having a safe place to stay for a week while Dirk was on a temporary restraining order. I felt I had to comply or be homeless. So, I told them about Dirk's watching pornography on the internet and expecting me to imitate what he had seen. I detailed some of his perverse sexual issues, and how I had probably enabled them by bringing his food and drinks to the computer whenever he demanded. I did what he wanted me to do. If I did otherwise, I knew the consequences would involve pain and bruises.

I could see the shock on their faces of what I had revealed to them. The pastor stated that I should have reported these to him and come forward to the altar after the Sunday morning church service and repented. His statements were a knife to my heart. "Since you participated, you should confess your sin to God and repent." *Repent? Had I sinned?*

Remembering the conditions of my staying at their house, I prayed, asking God to forgive me. I didn't know what else to say. I remembered the verse, "Likewise the Spirit also helpeth our infirmities: for we know not what we should pray for as we ought: but the Spirit itself maketh intercession for us with groanings which cannot be uttered," (Romans 8:26 KJV). God knew what I needed to say, even when I did not.

After the "amen," Joyce served brownies and coffee, and we made polite conversation. I had opened up to them as I never had to anyone before; I felt awkward and exposed. It seemed the others had dismissed my stark revelations only to discuss the weather and current events, sipping coffee as if it were a typical social visit. The pastor left, his parting words saying that he would pray for Dirk and me. Ally and I stayed with Mark and Joyce for the rest of the week.

The week did not go smoothly. Dirk called me demanding to see Ally. He threatened to have me arrested and charged with kidnapping if I did not allow him to see her. He told me he was coming to the house where I was staying. I reminded him that he was not allowed to go near me. He was so angry, cursing at me and threatening to have me arrested.

I was scared. I didn't know what to do, but I couldn't stay at the house. What if Dirk came? No one was home except Ally and me. What was I going to do? I went to the bedroom where our things were and got Ally's jacket. I buckled her into her car seat and said a prayer to God to keep us safe. I drove around town; I was afraid to stop anywhere. Dirk kept calling my phone to harass me. He wanted Ally. But I knew it wasn't safe for Dirk to see her or me. He had bragged that if I ever tried to leave him that he would use Ally against me. I realized this was a genuine threat. If the police arrested me, what would happen to her? The thoughts haunted me. *What will we do? Is there anywhere we can be safe? Where is God?*

After driving for an hour, Ally fell asleep in her car seat. I was thankful to God for that small blessing. I didn't think I could handle her crying. If she cried, I would melt into tears. I cautiously drove back to the elder's home and let myself inside. They were still at work. Dirk called one last time to yell at me for keeping Ally from him. I had called my counselor, who assured me that Dirk could not have me arrested, and that I should not talk to him while he was under the restraining order. When I reminded him that he was not to contact me because it violated the court order, he cursed angrily and hung up.

Later in the week, the pastor called me to set up a "mediation" meeting between Dirk and me. He prayed with us and sent us home together to work things out. Dirk had brought two of Ally's favorite toys, her colorful baby rings, and a Reese's Peanut Butter Cup for me as a token of apology. I wanted to believe the pastor. We had prayed together. But Dirk seemed disheveled, his hair was uncombed, his clothes were wrinkled and messy, and he was unshaven. Were these signs of his repentance? Had God answered my prayers?

I went home at the end of the week-long temporary restraining order. Dirk was sorry, and things were okay for a while. I made up excuses to go to the grocery store so I could be in a place where Dirk was not watching me. I sat in the grocery store parking lot to talk with friends on my cell phone and escape Dirk's intense scrutiny for a while. Of course, I never left Ally alone with him when she was awake. Unconvinced that Dirk knew how to care for her, I only left her during her naptime. I always returned before she awoke.

I returned from grocery shopping one afternoon and was putting the food away as Dirk called me over to his computer. He told me to "have a seat." I watched in horror as he created a website to show to the world my infidelity, including pictures of me. As he worked, he informed me of his plan to divorce me, leaving me with nothing. He tormented me with the way I did not fulfill the Biblical passages about the wife's duty to please the husband and obey him.

I felt guilty and ashamed, but I had given in to all his demands. Even when I had doubts, I tried to do everything he wanted me to do. Now my decision was public; all the world could see the website he had posted with the hope that others would make comments and support his position. Dirk designed this website to motivate others to investigate and harass me and anyone else who would still befriend me online or in person.

I was humiliated. My life was in ruins. I would never be able to teach anywhere, especially in a Christian school. I held back tears. Finally, he allowed me to leave his desk saying that he would call my parents to tell them about my affair and what a terrible person I was, or I could call them to speak to them first. At that moment, it seemed that divorce was the only option left. I could not keep the conflict from my parents any longer.

I immediately ran to our bedroom and sat on my side of the bed. Crying as I dialed, my mom picked up, and I told her of Dirk's plan for us to divorce.

"What did you do?" she accused. Her comment cut me to my core. *Why would my mom assume that I had done something?*

I explained that our marriage had been terrible for a long time. "I don't know what I'm going to do, Mom."

"Then you should fix it," she replied with finality.

I did not know how, or if there was any way, to fix things with Dirk, even though we had been married twelve years. I had thought deeply about the possibilities for Dirk's and my marriage.

To celebrate Valentine's Day, we had lunch at a restaurant overlooking Puget Sound. We talked about the weather, Ally, and our future as we enjoyed the view.

Dirk went silent when I changed the subject to our situation and shared my three conclusions. My first choice was that we could seek marital counseling and try to work things out. A second alternative would be to get a divorce immediately, but I didn't like that option at all. The last selection would be that we stay together for a year while I took the college classes and completed the paperwork to renew my teaching certificate, got a job, and became financially independent. Then we would divorce after the year.

Dirk was boiling! How dare I give him an ultimatum over Valentine's Day lunch in a restaurant. I didn't recognize my conclusions as being an ultimatum as much as the only logical choices to move forward. Ours was a silent ferry ride home. "Make plans that don't involve me," Dirk snarled.

"I need more time to renew my now-expired teaching certificate and save some money," I protested.

"I shouldn't have to pay for that! You're on your own."

The next morning, Dirk went to work. My mind rehashed our Valentine's Day conversation. *What had I said that would cause that tremendous irate response?* My counselor had made sure I knew the signs of an upcoming explosion, and Dirk seemed to be showing almost all of them. While he was out, I called my counselor to make an urgent appointment. I took Ally with me.

The counselor reiterated that Dirk could become violent and dangerous. I was scared. I had never seen him like this before and for so long. I thought he would snap out of it. But the counselor felt uneasy about sending me back home alone with Dirk "escalating" as she called it.

While I was at the counselor's office, her staff called Dirk's command to put him on a second temporary restraining order. Dirk was not to come to our apartment or have any contact with Ally or me for two weeks. He was being moved into a temporary barracks room by himself.

I knew Dirk would be infuriated. He hated the barracks, and he hated having to comply with the rules of living there. To make matters worse, he was not allowed to take his computer.

I went to a friend's home for two hours, at the request of Dirk's command, so that he could gather enough uniforms, clothing, and toiletries for the two weeks. The MPs would escort him to ensure he got what he needed and didn't destroy anything that didn't belong to him.

I took Ally home and made us dinner. I noticed how quiet and peaceful our home seemed. The quiet was shattered when I awoke to Ally's crying in the night. I went to her room to find her covered in green slime. I gagged as I realized I didn't know from which end the gunk had come. Poor baby! I wiped her down the best I could and took her to the bathroom to wash her. She hated baths, and this one was nasty.

I tried to be quick and efficient as I washed her from head to toe. She loved being snuggled after her bath, especially having the baby lotion rubbed on her back, arms, and legs. I relished the snuggles with my clean, happy baby girl.

I secured her in her swing and started the motor. She was content in her swing, and she was safe there for a few minutes while I stripped her bedding and put it in the washing machine. I set the dial to "hot" and "heavy dirt." I wasn't taking any chances on her blankets still being dirty.

As I put new sheets on her crib, I remembered Dirk saying that I was going to be a single parent soon. This situation with a sick baby had to be one of the worst for a single parent and, if I could deal with this one successfully, maybe life would be better without him? I pushed the thought aside; surely, God will miraculously fix our marriage, right? He is the God of miracles, after all. Even though Dirk wanted a divorce, I believed repairing our relationship had to be part of God's plan.

Early the next morning, Ally awoke with a fever. She had little red spots all over her body. I called the Ask-a-Nurse helpline for advice because I was unsure of what to do. I didn't remember reading anything about these spots in any of the baby care books. The nurse suggested Baby Motrin or Baby Tylenol. I gave her the medicine, but Ally did not feel better. She did not want to snuggle; she needed to sit on my lap.

Ally signed to me "ouch," the ASL symbol for pain and pointed to her spots. She had her one-year-old vaccinations the week before, and she had played with the other children at the Navy wives' activity, but no one had said anything about a rash.

Since she was so young and the fever did not go away, I took her to the clinic. The doctors were unable to diagnose the problem, but they gave me more potent pain medicine for her. Another day went by with Ally still miserable, so I called the clinic again.

A new doctor had arrived from San Diego; he would see Ally. He loved pediatric mysteries, according to his nurse. I was not to bring Ally into the hospital, so I waited in the parking lot of the emergency room. When it was our turn, the doctor and a nurse came out to see us. They wore masks and gloves. Taking a look at Ally's spots, he confirmed that she had measles.

"How did she get them?" I asked.

"Has she been in contact with anyone who has been overseas

or anyone you know with measles?"

"No," I could barely think. *Measles??*

The doctor paused. "Did she get the measles or the MMR shot in the last week or two?"

"Yes," I replied, "her one-year-old shots."

Laughingly the doctor continued, "Take this girl to Vegas; she's one in a million."

The new doctor explained that since measles had been mostly eradicated in the United States, Ally's regular doctor was unable to diagnose it. He identified it quickly because he had worked with undocumented immigrants in Southern California where measles outbreaks were becoming common.

The doctor gave me instructions to give Ally calming baths, popsicles, lots of liquids, and naps. But his last words were even more ominous. "She had the chickenpox shot with the measles one, right? Theoretically, she could develop chickenpox and measles at the same time. Those diseases are not mutually exclusive."

"You're saying that my child has measles but could get chickenpox, too?" *Was I hearing him correctly?* He nodded in affirmation.

The news was almost too much. I responded, "I'm all by myself. If Ally gets chickenpox along with the measles, we will need a hospital room. I'm not sure I can take care of her." He reassured me that I was doing fine, and Ally would get better.

The doctors quarantined Ally and me for two weeks. I called Carlee since Ally and I had visited her house the day before she broke out. We had unknowingly exposed her family to measles! I felt horrible about that, especially since Carlee and her family were moving to South Carolina. Moving with measles sounded miserable, and I could only hope they didn't catch it as they planned to spend the next week in the car sightseeing as they made the five-day drive to their new home. I apologized profusely, but Carlee graciously dismissed it, assuring me I had nothing to be sorry for. It wasn't like I had any control over this!

She brought us food from the grocery store, making sure we had everything we needed before she left. Dirk was staying in the barracks, but he had gone out to sea with his submarine for a short deployment. By the time he returned, Ally's measles had cleared up, and the second restraining order had expired. She did not get chickenpox, thank God!

Dirk and I talked sometimes, and things didn't feel so bad, but then, at other times, he continued badgering me to get to the point. He scolded me for wasting his time talking about stuff he didn't care about and had no interest in. He still wanted to get a divorce, but I hoped we could work things out. Our relationship felt okay, but certainly not improved enough for me to let my guard down. I beat myself up inside, trying to figure out how to please Dirk. Nothing made sense. Why did I make him so angry?

I was trying to save some money from our grocery bill each week in case I needed it to find a safe place away from Dirk. My teaching certificate renewal had hit a standstill. Because I graduated from a Christian college, I was not eligible for a teaching certificate in Washington. I would have to take almost four years of college all over again.

At another weekly meeting with my counselor, she asked, "Have you considered that you might not be the problem? What if you can't fix Dirk?"

I needed time to ponder that thought.

16. EXPLOSION

"If it be possible, as much as lieth in you, live peaceably with all men."
— Romans 12:18 KJV

April 26, 2006 was the day that tilted my universe. Dirk was still sleeping when I had left early that morning. He sat at his desk playing video games late into the night. He played in an online computer game for eight to twelve hours at a time every day, rarely leaving his computer chair except to use the bathroom. In order not to disrupt his gaming, Dirk would demand that I bring food and soda to him at the computer. Dirk became obsessed with the game currency, spending more and more time buying and selling in-game goods. I obeyed and delivered what he demanded. I was still in the mindset of being a dutiful wife.

That morning I awoke around 3:00 a.m. to find that Dirk was still in the office playing online games and surfing pornography. I sleepily walked out in my nightgown and asked him to come to bed, but he refused by saying, "I just need a few more transactions." I could tell that I was interrupting something by the way he quickly closed the pornography tab and shifted a pillow over his lap. His late-night activities were becoming an all-too-frequent routine.

After volunteering at a Navy wife mentoring seminar that morning, I arrived home to find sorted piles of our belongings. Dirk had instructed me several nights before to make a list of what I wanted from the apartment as we proceeded with our divorce. I had made a list, but he had created one of his own. He had decided what he would take and what I would be allowed to keep.

After putting Ally down to take a nap, I went into the bedroom to change into casual clothing when I noticed quite a few of my belongings were missing. Dirk sorted through everything I owned, sparing nothing. Unfeelingly and intrusively, he had sorted my jewelry, my clothes hanging in my closet, my cosmetics from the bathroom, and even my makeup and bathrobe. The most disturbing find was that he had taken some of my underwear, bras, and nightgowns.

When I confronted him, he snarled, "You don't deserve them. I'm taking them to put on my *new* girlfriend. While I was on the last restraining order, I had a woman hit on me at a restaurant. I'll give them to the next woman to share our bed. The bed won't be cold before I find someone else."

Eyeing my sewing kit that was sitting on my desk, he promptly dumped the contents. He knew that my grandmother had given it to me for sewing and mending emergencies before she had passed away. Dirk said, "I need it." I couldn't believe his cruelty. I thought that he loved me.

The unimaginable malice continued as he rifled through my desk drawer. "You have two calculators. I want one; choose which one you want." I picked the one my principal had given me as a teacher appreciation gift. Knowing its sentimental value, Dirk hurled the calculator against the wall. I watched as it smashed into pieces! "I recommend you take the other one since that one's broken." I cringed under his scrutiny. I didn't dare leave the bedroom until he allowed it. I knew the consequences!

Mercilessly, Dirk continued searching my desk drawers. He brutishly held up the treasured letter from my favorite aunt, saying how proud she was of the good Christian woman I had become. She had written it a month before she had died tragically in the car accident. "You'll get back this letter from your dead aunt when I get what I want. You don't *deserve* any of it."

Incredulously, I looked around the apartment, my mind frantically searching for my belongings. So many things from my list were missing. Refusing to tell me where they were, Dirk said he took what he deserved. Heartlessly, he rationalized that he needed those things since he would be living on his own. I held back tears, fearing my response would result in my having more bruises.

Dirk recalled, "Now I know why my father threw my mother over a fence into a pool and hit her. She didn't listen to him—just like you don't listen." I thought to myself, *and because I didn't submit to his every sadistic sexual fantasy.*

I couldn't help but sob, however, and beg him for my missing clothes and jewelry. Everything I had once thought was right, kind, loving, and moral about our relationship was in shambles.

Dirk was pacing now. Afraid for my life, I went into the kitchen and called Rhonda, my Navy wife liaison—the first step in my escape plan if I ever needed it.

I heard violent crashing in our bedroom, and then Dirk came into the kitchen, where I was on the phone waiting for Rhonda to answer. Furious to see the phone in my hand, he angrily questioned, "Who are you calling? Are you calling to have me removed? I'm not going under another restraining order. I'm staying right here!" Then, oddly, he demanded, "Kiss me goodbye! I'm leaving forever." I did not dare disobey, so I complied. I kissed Dirk goodbye.

As he stalked out of the room, I turned back toward the kitchen window. I thought he would follow through with his typical behavior pattern—go pout or wait a while before coming back to say, "You made me angry." Any dispute was always my fault.

As Rhonda answered, I screamed! Dirk suddenly grabbed the back of my neck in one hand and my right arm with his other hand. "I'm not leaving this apartment! You are!" he snarled.

Struggling to hold the phone to my ear, I heard Rhonda ask, "Are you okay?" Without waiting for an answer, she added, "I'm calling 911. Help will be on the way." I barely heard her say to the operator that she was listening to domestic violence taking place. "I'm hearing someone on the telephone being hurt." While talking to the operator, Rhonda kept reassuring me that help was coming.

Dirk quickly picked me up. I stretched as hard as I could, but my feet could not touch the floor as he hauled me the few steps to the doorway. He opened our metal front door and slammed me ferociously into the glass storm door. "You need to leave. I'm making sure you go!" He thrust me into the door a second time. Fearing for my life, I frantically struggled to get it open and escape his wrath.

When he smashed my face against the glass door a third time, my left arm went through the lower screen of the door. I used my right arm to cover my face as best I could. Panicking, I pulled my hand out of the screen and struggled to find the latch without looking. I didn't want to know if I could survive a fourth hit against the door.

I finally found the handle, and the door miraculously opened. Held fast in Dirk's solid grip, I had no way to escape. With one hand savagely gripping the back of my neck, and the other on my right upper arm, he hurled me through the doorway.

I struggled to land one foot on the top landing. I did not touch any of the other twelve stair steps. On the bottom stair landing, I whispered a quick prayer, "Thank You, God!" as I landed on my feet and ran.

I hid behind the dumpsters in the dirty trash enclosure by the garage. Terrified, I listened as Dirk came down the stairs snarling threats at me. "You're going to pay for making me put up with you!"

Somehow I had managed to hold on to the cell phone as he had thrown me from the apartment. I held the phone to my ear and heard Rhonda's voice as she calmly assured me that, "Help is on the way." I did not dare to respond. I cried desperate, silent tears. Despite her assurances, my mind screamed unanswered questions. *Where are my neighbors? Can no one hear me? Isn't anyone coming to help me?*

I heard Dirk continue his angry rant about "not another restraining order." I listened to him stomp up the stairs into our apartment. The door slammed!

As I peeked cautiously through the gaps between the boards of the trash enclosure, I heard him throw open the door and watched as he jogged down the stairs while triumphantly holding up my car keys. "I'm taking your car. You get nothing. You get nothing. I deserve it because I put up with you." In silence, I wiped away uncontrollable tears.

Still cowering in my hiding place behind the trash dumpsters, I shouted, "Ally is sleeping. What if I need to take her to the doctor or something?" That question seemed to cause him to pause. He threw down my keys.

I heard Dirk's truck engine rev and the tires squeal. I peeked timidly through the fence as he sped away. I made sure he was gone before I dashed back up the stairs to check on Ally. Miraculously, she was still napping. I finished getting dressed and sat on the couch crying and hoping help would arrive soon. I was stunned and shocked by what had just happened.

The MPs and Rhonda arrived at the same time. As the MPs waited for an ambulance, they made sure Dirk had driven off. "Do you think he tried to kill you?" was the first question. I had been married to him for twelve years. I had never even considered the thought that he would try to kill me. *Had he wanted to kill me?* I asked myself. "No," I answered automatically. *He couldn't have, right?*

As an EMT, emergency medical technician, checked me over, the MPs asked what had happened. After I explained it to them, the MPs took pictures of everything in the apartment. It was now considered a crime scene. *Do I live in a crime scene?*

I told the officers about the previous restraining orders, my counselor, and Dirk's access to weapons. The EMTs cataloged my injuries. I had a cut over my eye, bruises on my neck and arms, and I hurt inside and out. "I'll be fine," I assured them. I was in denial.

The EMTs advised me to go to the hospital, but I did not want to ride in the ambulance. *What would I do with my baby girl?* My friend Chloe, who had arrived sometime during the questioning, insisted she would drive me to the hospital. She convinced me to go to the emergency room. I didn't take anything with me except Ally's diaper bag. I thought we would be coming right back home.

Chloe put my daughter's car seat in her car, and we left for the hospital. I closed my eyes during the drive. My head throbbed as I began thinking about how I did not believe my counselor when she had said that Dirk might explode and hurt me. *How could a Christian man possibly do that?* I had wondered. Ignorantly, I had replied, "Dirk would never hurt me. He loves me."

I never imagined I would have to use the safety plan I made with my counselor. However, unknown to me, my counselor had set up a social worker, Navy Criminal Investigative Service (NCIS) detectives, and doctors who were ready to help me when the explosion happened.

The EMTs had called ahead to the hospital so that everyone, the emergency room doctors, the social worker, and NCIS detectives, were all ready for my arrival. Chloe said, "I'll play with Ally in the waiting room." It all seemed so surreal.

At the hospital, a nurse escorted me to a private room behind the emergency department, where she put a brace on my neck. "You are in a safe place," she reassured me. As part of their domestic violence victim protocol, the authorities would refuse to communicate any information about my whereabouts to Dirk.

The nurse helped me into a wheelchair to roll me to the radiology department, where the technicians took extensive x-rays of my head and neck. I did not feel any of the injuries. Emotionally, my mind could not come to terms with the thought that someone who had said he loved me could ever treat me like this.

Once the doctors reviewed the x-rays, they determined that I did not have any broken bones, but I would have to wear a neck brace. The nurses then treated the cut over my eye and my left arm for the injuries caused by the screen. I felt emotionally detached the entire time they attended to my lacerations.

After the doctors and nurses determined that I didn't have any life-threatening injuries, the NCIS detectives were allowed to question me. The detectives kindly asked if there was anyone I should call. I wasn't sure but, finally, I decided to call my parents. I gave my mother a quick synopsis of what had happened. "Dirk threw me out of the apartment and down the concrete stairs, but somehow God helped me land on my feet. I am in the emergency room, and doctors are checking me over. I don't think I have any broken bones."

"What did you do?" she asked. I was stunned by this first question my mom asked. They loved Dirk and admired his being in the Navy, but I was her daughter, and he had *hurt* me.

Astounded by her immediate response, I told her I must hang up to speak with the doctor who had come into my room. *How could my mother ask what I did to cause this brutal attack? How can she think I did something to deserve this?*

The doctor had come to my room to check in with me and relay the final x-ray results. I had no broken bones that they could see, but I would be very sore and probably unable to sleep. He prescribed pain killers and sleeping pills for me. I had never taken such strong medications before. Did I need them?

After the doctor left my room, the NCIS detectives asked more questions about my injuries. The male detectives took pictures cataloging each wound. I felt so humiliated as they made numerous photos of my battered face, my scratched left arm, the emerging bruises on my right arm, and the developing bruise line across my thighs.

They took close-up pictures of the cut over my right eye, which was developing into a black eye. The images revealed that I had hit the door with significant momentum. More photos of the bruises on my neck and right arm demonstrated Dirk's ferocity. Within a few days, the injuries on the back of my neck and my right arm developed into perfect imprints of Dirk's hands. I almost felt as if I were watching all this happen to another person rather than to my own body.

After several hours, the hospital staff, the social worker, and the NCIS detectives decided I was allowed to leave—but not allowed to go home. The detectives explained that Dirk was possibly armed and extremely dangerous. They had not found him yet, so I needed a place to go.

Chloe offered to let us spend the night at her house. Concerned, the detectives questioned if she could keep us safe. They asked if she could hide my car from view. Chloe explained, "My husband is on duty at sea so that I can hide her car in the garage. I also have a gun. I can camouflage the car and keep them safe for the night." With only the clothes on my back and a diaper bag for Ally, we left for Chloe's home.

When would my church friends reach out to help us? My mind was reeling.

17. HIDING

"Thou art my hiding place and my shield: I hope in thy word."
— Psalm 119:114 KJV

Chloe's husband, Craig, was out to sea on a long deployment. Until Dirk was arrested and lost his security clearance, he and Craig served aboard the same submarine. Chloe said we could stay with her and her four daughters until the end of Craig's deployment. We took over the girls' bedroom with bunk beds. I slept on the bottom bunk next to Ally, who slept in a playpen. I kept it in the trunk of my car as part of my "just in case" preparations. Thankfully, we had a place to live for the next three months. I hoped we wouldn't have to stay that long.

On my first day at Chloe's house, Amanda, another one of my Navy wife friends, came by to ask what I needed. Chloe had called her since we were all friends. I explained to Amanda that I only had the clothes I was wearing and two changes of clothes for Ally in the diaper bag. Everything I owned was in our apartment, but I was not allowed to go there at all, not even to get clothes. Our home was unsafe since Navy regulations did not let the NCIS detectives take Dirk's keys as the Navy required only his name on our apartment lease. Because it was rented in his name, I was effectively homeless.

Amanda brought me to Target to shop while Chloe stayed at home to watch Ally. Amanda purchased pajamas, underwear, and a pantsuit for court for me, along with a couple of sets of clothes and diapers for Ally. She said, "It's the least I can do," as she gave me a side hug. We went to the Starbucks drive-through. She said I needed a good hot tea, and she wanted coffee before we got back to Chloe's.

I had not heard anything from my church friends, but some non-Christian Navy wives were helping me. *Where were my Christian friends? Would they know what was happening to me?*

I felt relatively safe at Chloe's house, but when I tried to sleep, I woke in a panic having nightmares of Dirk. My mind was full of questions. *How could God allow this to happen to me? What did I do? I tried my best to be a good wife.* I believed, according to the Bible, that divorce was a serious matter. I honestly presumed that God would help me understand my husband and make our relationship better. Didn't God do miracles for other people? I had done everything I could think of to save my marriage, things I didn't even want to do, something that made me feel small, dirty, and degraded. I had submitted to my husband in all things, hadn't I? He, as the head of the household, made the final decisions. Besides, I was a military wife. I knew my place. *Why was my marriage ending this way?* I had always been a "good" Christian woman. Where was God?

I had not heard anything from my church friends. I was sure Dirk had called them and our pastor and told them about my affair and what a bad wife I had been all this time. I had expected to get a call from the deacon's wife who hosted Ally's baby shower and took me shopping at the mall, or from the ladies who had invited me over for tea and Bible study to at least call to check on me. But there was no one.

Some of my non-Christian Navy wife friends were helping me. I wondered, *"Where are my Christian friends?"*

18. ADVOCATE

*"Remember now thy Creator in the days of thy youth, while the evil days
come not, nor the years draw nigh when thou shalt say, I have no pleasure in
them."*
- Ecclesiastes 12:1 KJV

Dirk had told the arresting officers he would "finish the job."
The detectives believed him. They had reports of his truck being
seen at our church's parking lot late at night and driving by the
homes of ladies he knew as my friends. He used the phone
numbers from my call history on our phone bill to call as many of
my friends as he could, telling them that I had left him for
someone else. He was looking for me, stalking me, and harassing
anyone who would still admit to being friend with me.

Although detectives considered Dirk armed and dangerous and
a threat to my life, his command continued to allow him to go
wherever he liked. The authorities believed that Dirk would try to
kill me again. I could not live with him; it was too dangerous.

Still in hiding, I continued faithfully attending my counseling
sessions. These appointments were necessary to ensure my safety.
The detectives called them "health checks," because they were
absolutely sure that Dirk would try to kill me again.

After Dirk's explosion, the Navy Family Advocacy Program
assigned me a domestic violence advocate named Susan. I met
with her in addition to my weekly counseling session. Susan

immediately made me feel calm despite the circumstances that brought me to her office. She was an older lady with gray hair, a bit heavier than she would have liked, she joked, and pleasant. She introduced herself as a Christian and a Bible-believer who became an advocate because her ex-husband beat her so severely that she had spent weeks in the intensive care unit at the hospital. She divorced him and remarried her current husband who she said was a "gem." He was the man she had always dreamed existed for her.

In the midst of all of this chaos, I felt relieved to finally speak with someone who shared my Christian faith and desire to please God. With her, I felt comfortable enough to ask previously "forbidden" questions and get honest answers from a Christian point of view, even if it was a different opinion than I had heard at my church. One of our first conversation topics was the idea of marriage and divorce. Susan, like me, had always been taught that "The Lord God of Israel says that He hates divorce," (Malachi 2:16 NKJV). I had always been taught that divorce is never the answer for any reason. But what was I to do? I was living in constant fear and abuse. In contrast, Susan challenged me with the idea that God doesn't want his children to be harmed, especially by the husband. Wasn't the command, "Husbands, love your wives, even as Christ also loved the church, and gave himself for it;" (Ephesians 5:25 KJV)?

Susan explained how she had come to her decision to get divorced. She realized that God loved her and wanted her to be safe. When her husband beat her, he had broken their marriage vows "to love, honor and cherish" his wife. He had also broken God's command, "Husbands, love your wives, even as Christ also loved the church, and gave himself for it," (Ephesians 5:25 KJV). Abuse is never a part of God's commands.

While Susan was speaking, it seemed God touched my heart. Dirk had broken our marriage vows. The law enforcement officials believed that he would try to kill me. How could I stay in a marriage where I would be in grave danger? Should I stay with a man who wouldn't hesitate to hurt me? That wasn't loving. Is this something that God would want for my daughter and me? It couldn't be part of God's plan for my marriage.

In Washington State the authorities prosecute any crime labeled as domestic violence. The victim cannot decide whether or not to press charges which alleviates the stress and blame on them. I was grateful for that because, in my fragile state, it would have been difficult for me to press charges and go through all the court proceedings. But the court case was already in process; I received a protection order.

But, divorce? What was I to do? I knew what my mother thought. She had made that clear by asking, "What did you do?" and declaring, "you need to fix this!" I knew what the church thought. I heard it my entire life. I even knew what would happen to my teaching career in Christian schools and churches, at least within my denomination. I had seen it. I would never be allowed to teach in those schools or churches again. I would be an outcast with a scarlet letter. No one would consider the reason. My life as I knew it was in shambles.

I had nothing left. No home, no job, no church family, few friends, little money, and no way to earn any more. I felt emotionally exhausted and completely overwhelmed with the feelings of being utterly stuck and the despair of never being able to have anything better. I gave up hope that God would fix my marriage. My last hope was that He would keep me alive and safe to be able to raise my daughter. My prayers became: *God give me the strength to get through today*. It was all I could manage.

The choice became clear: divorce or death. I chose divorce.

19. NCIS

"And ye shall know the truth, and the truth shall make you free." –
John 8:32 KJV

I was still recovering from my injuries when the NCIS detectives summoned me to their headquarters for questioning. Susan, my domestic violence advocate, met me at the NCIS detective's office. She held my hand and reassured me, "You are safe with them. Tell them everything you have been through."

They labeled my case, *Domestic Violence Assault*. One of the detectives read the arrest report detailing how the MPs had apprehended Dirk while trying to return to our apartment late on the night after he assaulted me. During questioning, he reported he had gone to the bank to withdraw half of the money from the sale of our condo. Then he had gone to a Red Lobster restaurant to have dinner by himself in peace and, later on, to watch a movie.

While being questioned, Dirk had stated calmly that, if he found me, he would "finish the job." This declaration, along with my previous statements, disturbed the detectives. As a result, they continued to call me daily to take "health check" measures ensuring that Dirk hadn't located where I was staying. They considered my life in grave danger.

As part of my safety plan, my counselor instructed me to "keep my phone on my person at all times." I had to call to let the MPs know that I was going from Chloe's home on the Navy base to see my counselor. When I arrived at my counselor's office, the secretary called the MPs to let them know I was there. I called Chloe to let her know I had arrived safely.

After my appointment, the secretary called the MPs again to tell them that I was leaving, and I called Chloe to let her know I would be coming back to the house. All these communication procedures were to keep me safe from Dirk—and alive.

I was exhausted after answering their questions for over eight hours on the first day. However, since their original questions provoked more questions, I was scheduled for another full day. I spent another eight hours the second day answering more questions and trying to comprehend how my life had come to bruises, meeting with counselors, and answering detectives' questions about my husband. Detectives took more pictures of my injuries, cataloging them as they developed more conspicuously. I felt numb and detached from these proceedings as if I were watching someone else's life instead of participating in my own.

I will never forget two of the numerous questions the detectives asked. "Did Dirk ever leave bruises on you before this? Have you ever left bruises on Dirk?" I felt horrified. *Am I guilty of assaulting Dirk?* I didn't know how to explain all that I had endured. I watched as these men painstakingly recorded all of my responses in detail.

Numbed by all the trauma, I told them of the numerous times that Dirk would grab my breasts or bottom and tickle me. The playful touching led to his wrestling me to the floor as I protested by saying, "No, stop! NO!"

His so-called tickling was painful and usually left bruises. As he held me down, he wouldn't stop saying, "You'll like it once I get inside you." I explained that he repeated this same statement every time he wrestled me down.

"I tried to fight back and to stop him. Most of the time, I gave up," I explained. Feeling self-conscious and ashamed, I bowed my head to avoid eye contact. "Yes, I probably left bruises on his arms and legs when I fought back." In my confusion and shock, I couldn't stop thinking, *Was I guilty of abusing him? Was Dirk right? Was everything my fault?*

The detectives gently explained that any marks I left on Dirk were self-defense. They continued, "When a woman says 'no' or 'stop,' the man has a legal responsibility to stop, and that includes married men." They stated clearly, "When he doesn't stop, the act is considered rape." *Even in marriage!*

This declaration rocked my world! Had my husband repeatedly raped me? He had forced me to please him sexually several times a day. I had been conditioned to believe that I would not be a good Christian wife if I did not do everything my husband commanded—no matter what I thought of it. I had told him "no" and told him to stop when he did things I didn't like. I had tried to tell him how much I hated so many of his fantasies, and that I didn't want to participate. I had been clear. I had a lot of thinking to do. *It was rape.*

The NCIS detectives informed Dirk's shore command of the seriousness of my situation. Dirk was considered "armed and dangerous" with "intent" to harm me. The detectives suggested placing Dirk on house arrest in the barracks with constant supervision, but his new commanding officer refused. Dirk had convinced his commander that I was just a delusional Navy wife having an illicit affair. According to him, we were going through a nasty divorce, and I was "making up drama." Dirk was free to come and go as he wished, but I had to remain in hiding and in fear for my life.

And there was nothing I could do about it.

20. DESPAIR

"The LORD redeemeth the soul of his servants; none of them that trust in Him shall be desolate."
– Psalm 34:22 KJV

On a sunny afternoon, Chloe and I watched as Ally and her girls played in their backyard. Ally ran, giggling and squealing with joy, as the girls playfully chased after her. She was so loud. As instinct kicked in, I shushed her as I always had before when I was fearful that she might disturb Dirk. Hearing me, Chloe called, "Remember? You're not there anymore. Ally's just having fun. Let her play."

I realized this was the first time I'd ever heard my little girl laugh freely with delight. She was almost two years old.

During the day, Ally played with the girls while Chloe and I watched them. Chloe gave me some books to read as a distraction from my troubles. She taught me some of her favorite recipes as we prepared dinner. I could not renew my teaching certificate, look for an apartment, or even find a job. The detectives thought it was too dangerous. They believed Dirk was looking for me and, if I was to escape with my life, I must remain in hiding.

In the evenings, after we put the girls to bed, we stayed up watching girly movies and chatting. Being with her was a good distraction amid a terrible situation. Chloe lived in a quiet cul-de-sac with very little traffic, and she had lived there so long she knew all the neighbors. However, in that quiet neighborhood, we would hear vehicles drive slowly by her house almost every night. We didn't think anything about the unusual amount of traffic and assumed the neighbors were coming home late.

How wrong we were.

Late one night, when we heard a vehicle driving unusually slow several times past Chloe's house, she decided to peek cautiously out the window. Moving the curtain ever so slightly, she spotted Dirk's truck canvassing the neighborhood. My mind shrieked, *He's looking for me!*

Chloe had hidden my car in her garage behind Craig's truck and her car. There was no way Dirk would see it unless he got out of his vehicle to look in the garage windows. Chloe asked, "Do you think I should get my pistol?"

I was so petrified that I could not reply. Dirk made several slower passes of Chloe's house, but he did not stop. We sat on the couch in silence, waiting for the worst imaginable confrontation with Dirk.

What was I to do? Where would I go? In a few weeks, Chloe's husband would be coming home from his three-month deployment. We could no longer stay there safely. Ally and I needed a different place to stay. NCIS detectives said we could not rent an apartment; they were afraid that Dirk would discover our whereabouts and hurt us. I visited my closest church friends in the hope that someone would help us.

Bruised, desperate, and homeless, I stood on the back porch of the head elder of my church who didn't invite me inside. My not-quite two-year-old daughter was in my car. I begged him for a place to stay in hiding from my soon-to-be ex-husband.

"I'm sorry," he said, "we've helped you as much as we can; he's dangerous. I'll pray for you." Rejected, with no hope left, I walked away. I couldn't believe what I was hearing!

I could not attend our small Baptist church for fear that Dirk would be there. He parked his truck at the church several nights in a row. Church friends reported Dirk driving slowly by their houses as if to spy on them or catch a glimpse of Ally or me after dark. My inner circle of church friends had seemingly abandoned me.

When Dirk was transferred from the submarine, I was no longer part of the boat's wives' group, and I lost their support. Besides, Dirk had made sure to tell all their husbands that I was crazy and having an affair. Most of my Navy wife friends didn't want any part of that drama, especially since I was no longer eligible to be part of that support group. I was alone with my daughter.

In desperation, I called the women's shelters for victims of domestic violence. I received the disheartening news that they were full and had no room for us. *Where were we to go? Had everyone abandoned us?*

21. UNEXPECTED HELP

"The righteous considereth the cause of the poor…"
— Proverbs 29:7 KJV

Fortunately, God spoke to the heart of an older lady from my church. Her name was Alice. Her family was on the fringe of the church congregation, but she heard of our predicament and took us in.

Our pastor and the inner church circle looked down on this family, even though Alice was the church treasurer. Alice's husband rarely attended church, and her unmarried daughter had a teenage son. They did not participate in every service. But in my time of desperate need, they opened their home to Ally and me.

Understanding that Dirk was dangerous and not wanting him to know my whereabouts, Alice's husband hid my car behind their barn and covered it with a tarp. We ate family dinner with them and had devotions after the meal. My illusions of them "not being spiritual enough" were quickly dispelled.

During this time I continued seeing my counselor, who was part of a Navy Family Service Center team that met to review potential abuse cases. After reviewing my case files and the evidence, this professional committee determined that I had been sexually, emotionally, physically, and verbally abused. I received an official letter stating their conclusions.

My counselor and domestic violence victim advocate

recommended that I read a particular book. I like to read, so I agreed. I had the time and needed a distraction. Except, this book was NOT a distraction. It was my life in words that I did not yet know how to express. Others had been through similar situations, and had come through it.

One afternoon as I sat on Alice's couch reading the book my counselor had given to me. Alice handed me a cup of tea and wondered aloud if I might feel comfortable sharing a bit of what my life had been like. Could we talk so that she would better know how to help me? Alice sat calmly in her rocking chair across the coffee table from me. Ally was napping.

I shared about Dirk's constant sex drive and need to control my every action right down to what I should wear. As I revealed details of the last few months of my married life, Alice began to cry. I was shocked by her response. *Why is she crying over what has happened to me?!* I had grown more accustomed to acknowledging what I now realized as abuse. I couldn't quite believe that my world was so twisted. Dirk had skillfully conditioned me to his whims and distorted thinking.

Alice asked if she could hug me. I could feel her sobbing as I opened up. Even though she was kind, I didn't dare tell her more for fear that she would think worse of me. As if she could read my thoughts, she put her arm around my shoulders to assure me that she and her family loved me and, more important than them, God loved me, too.

Later in the same week my pastor called. I was sitting in Alice's backyard screened-in gazebo watching Ally happily pick flowers and play with her toys. He told me that I needed to reconcile with Dirk. He reminded me that the Bible says God hates divorce; therefore, I should forgive Dirk and take him back.

He continued his message saying that we needed to confess our sins and go to counseling with him. I began to cry. I reminded him that I had taken Dirk back twice, despite the apparent dangers. For Ally's safety and mine, he had been served two separate restraining orders. Besides, Washington State was pressing charges for domestic violence and assault.

"Pastor, I cannot take him back. He tried to kill me," I insisted, being as blunt as I could.

The pastor then presented an ultimatum. "You must reconcile with Dirk, or we will vote to remove you from the membership of the church."

They would discipline me out. He was threatening to excommunicate me from the church. I knew this to be the ultimate consequence used only on people who were unrepentantly living in sin. I had trusted my pastor to share God's message. How could he think that I should reconcile with Dirk? *I have bruises, but I need to take Dirk back?* The thoughts screamed through my mind in disbelief.

"What?" I exclaimed. "How could you do such a thing? He has been abusing me for years. He viciously hurt me, and he could have killed me." I began sobbing into the phone again.

The pastor insisted I needed to ask God and Dirk to forgive my sins. "You must take Dirk back," he insisted.

Pushed to the limit, I responded, "Pastor, do whatever you feel you need to do. I'm leaving Washington State the minute the judge says I can, and I'm never coming back!"

The truth is, I was horrified at the thought of being excommunicated, but I was more terrified of Dirk.

I remembered the NCIS detective's face looking very serious as he said, "A piece of paper won't stop a bullet or bat." Even though I had a restraining order against Dirk, he had managed to violate it by threatening my mother, my friends, and anyone else brave enough to help me, telling them he knew where they lived and would find me to "finish this."

Although it sounded like common sense, they told me I *must* take care of myself. My daughter needed one safe, sane parent, and I was it! Susan stressed the idea of keeping my safety plan in action. At her recommendation, I kept my cell phone either on me or in my purse, where I could reach it at all times. My phone charged at night on my nightstand next to my pillow and was always within reach. I never silenced my phone. Some nights I fell asleep clutching it in my hand.

A second suggestion was to have a trusted friend call to check on me every day. One of the detectives, my advocate, or my counselor called me daily. Susan encouraged me, "If you see Dirk and feel threatened, or he confronts you, run away! Go to a place with lots of people. Don't be afraid to call 911 for help. Get away and get safe." Work the plan, she reiterated.

If I was out shopping or in a restaurant, I should make sure I knew where the exits were so I could get to them quickly. To get help, I should yell "fire" to get people's attention. If I screamed "help," people may not want to be involved, but they would respond to "fire."

I was beginning to grasp the level of danger I was facing. My morning and bedtime prayer became, "God, will I survive this?"

22. WAITING

"Anyone who withholds kindness from a friend forsakes the fear of the Almighty." - Job 6:14 NIV

God used Alice to keep Ally and me safe. I contacted former friends from the East Coast with my new phone number and situation. I heard from a married couple who had graduated with me from the seminary. He had agreed to pastor a small church near Alice's home. He invited me to attend. He assured me that I would be safe at his church.

The idea that a church would invite and even welcome me when I was in the middle of a domestic violence mess and divorcing my husband was utterly unsettling, given how I had been treated elsewhere. Not wanting to cause a scene, I arrived early to speak privately with the pastor and his wife. They met me at the front doors of the church with a hug.

Their compassion deeply moved me. In kindness, the pastor and his wife shared with me that, although God hates divorce, He wants His children to be safe. They continued, "The Lord also will be a refuge for the oppressed, a refuge in times of trouble," (Psalm 9:9 KJV).

I continued living in hiding with Alice and her family. I read books about domestic violence. But I was having difficulty reading my Bible and praying. I wondered what God had in store for Ally and me. What were we going to do?

During our separation and domestic violence court hearings,

for my safety, I was told to use a back entrance to the courthouse to arrive and leave at a specified time. A bailiff escorted me to a private room where Dirk could not see me before or after the procedure to avoid any ugly confrontations.

In the courtroom, I was accompanied by my attorney and Susan, my advocate. We sat behind a column out of Dirk's direct line of sight. Dirk had positioned himself where he hoped to intimidate me with stares of contempt. My attorney noticed his posture and mentioned it to the judge who called an extra bailiff as a guard into the courtroom, just in case. Facing the judge's bench, I prayed that God would direct the judge to let Ally and me go.

Dirk represented himself. He ranted about his need for the washer and dryer but did not ask for custody of Ally. Dirk only wanted her to visit with him. He had promised me he would use her to control me, and it seemed his plan was working. I had little choice. The judge decided. No, we could not leave the state.

Because Dirk was stationed there in Washington State, with no evidence of his hurting Ally, the judge ordered supervised visitations. I agreed to allow our pastor to supervise for financial reasons, and the judge agreed.

In a divorce involving children, it is customary that the parents are court-ordered to attend a parenting class, and the *guardian ad litem* must interview them. The *guardian ad litem* is the court's advocate for the child and is appointed by the judge. Our guardian interviewed me and several of my friends. She watched my interactions with Ally as she played with her toys on Chloe's living room floor.

As part of the interview with the guardian, we discussed finances. Dirk had left me some money that would allow me to get a place of my own and tide me over until I found a job if I kept a strict budget. My parents had agreed to help financially, too, just until I got back on my feet. Next, the guardian also interviewed Dirk, his friends, and our pastor. The final report showed that Dirk lacked parenting skills and did not attend the court-mandated parenting class.

The judge granted me full custody of Ally along with the

washer and dryer. However, I still was not allowed to leave the state; the judge granted Dirk supervised visitation.

23. MOVING OUT

"And I will deliver thee out of the hand of the wicked, and I will redeem thee out of the hand of the terrible." – Jeremiah 15:21 KJV

Our apartment was a mess--a crime-scene disaster-type mess--when I arrived to claim what was left of my belongings. Since I was not allowed to be there without an MP escort, I had arranged in advance for my three remaining Navy wives friends and their husbands to help me. My parents had flown in despite their initial reluctance to the idea of my getting a divorce. My mom was watching Ally to keep her out of the chaos.

The evening before the move, my parents came to Chloe's home to have dinner with us. They had gotten off the airplane and driven to a hotel nearby, but I could not stay with them. It was not safe.

As soon as he saw me, my dad pulled me into his arms and hugged me with an "I love you, Hun." My mom was more stand-offish. I hugged her and kissed her cheek. We talked about how Ally was growing, clearly avoiding the reason for their visit. My mom noticed my bruised arm, black eye, and the laceration over my eye. She asked if they hurt, but it had been almost a month. They didn't.

After dinner, as my parents talked with Chloe about the weather, current events, and made small talk, I went to my room to get my copy of the police report written by the detectives. I wanted my mother to read it, hoping she would believe that what

Dirk had done to me was not my fault. I wanted her to acknowledge my remaining shred of dignity and show compassion.

She sat in the rocking chair next to the picture window in Chloe's living room and opened the file folder. I watched as she read intently; she wore pained expressions as comprehension dawned. As she closed the papers, she said, "I'm sorry." At least she had read the facts, not just my side of the story. I felt better about her having a more objective picture of what had happened to me. It was nice to know she finally knew the truth.

When moving day arrived, we went to the apartment and waited outside as the MPs rechecked the place. Once again, they opened every closet and drawer and patted the cushions before we sat down. When we entered, I could tell Dirk had been in the apartment. If he showed up this particular day, he would be arrested and thrown in jail. I didn't think he would risk it, but I couldn't be sure.

I was an emotional wreck leading up to moving day, barely eating, and hardly sleeping. I was sick to my stomach at the whole idea of being back there, the scene of my assault, vividly realizing how many times I had been attacked and raped—here, where I should have been safe and loved. Overflowing emotions made me physically ill.

As the feelings swirled and threatened to overwhelm me, I tried to push them down to think about later. With only eight hours to get everything I owned packed up and put in a storage unit, I didn't have the time to fall apart now.

I gave my friends instructions and showed them the lists of what to pack and what to leave for Dirk. I had sorted some of my belongings on previous brief visits, but I was not allowed enough time to prepare anything before this day arrived.

As Mom played with Ally, I could tell she was stressed. Her phone rang; she motioned to me to get her a piece of paper and pen. She wrote, "It's Dirk." He launched into a diatribe about what a terrible person I was. Then he added, "Tell her I'm coming for her."

"Dirk, you are under a restraining order. Stop calling, or I will press charges." She repeated it several times. Finally, at Chloe's insistence, my mom hung up in tears.

We encouraged her to call the MPs who were standing guard outside. They asked her to write an official statement. They intended to find Dirk to warn him again. No contact meant NO contact—especially conveying messages through people he knew would be with me.

As my Navy friends and I cleaned up the apartment and packed my things, I had to stick to the court-approved list of items I could take. Dirk wanted the dining room table but not the matching hutch. He wanted the bed. I vividly recalled all the times he told me he would need it for his next woman. I didn't want it anyway. It held too many negative memories.

As we continued packing, I noticed I was missing so many items—my bathrobe, my favorite bras and underwear, my favorite dresses, sweaters, and nightgowns, even some of Ally's toys were gone. *So much for Dirk not being allowed to come to the apartment,* I thought.

Why? Why did he need my underwear and bras? My nightgowns? Would he give them to his next woman? Thoughts of his violation overwhelmed me as I packed the remaining clothing Dirk had left in a suitcase and boxes. I finally dismissed the feelings; I didn't have time to think about all that now. I needed to get out of there with what was left of my belongings.

All of the neighbors seemed to have disappeared as we packed the moving truck. The neighborhood was silent and eerily empty for a weekday afternoon. Apparently, we were the only ones around. We followed in our car as a friend drove the moving truck to the storage unit I had rented.

With a quick, silent prayer of thanks and desperation, I took a last look at my old life. I hoped for better days ahead, but I couldn't see an end to any of it. Trying to remain calm, I prayed, "Casting all your care upon Him, for he careth for you," (I Peter 5:7 KJV).

I wondered what would happen next.

24. LEAVING

"There hath no temptation taken you but such as is common to man: but God is faithful, who will not suffer you to be tempted above that ye are able; but will with the temptation also make a way to escape, that ye may be able to bear it."– I Corinthians 10:13 KJV

As I continued numerous appointments with my advocate, counselor, and lawyer, Dirk was ordered to undergo psychological testing because of the Navy counselors' findings that I had suffered abuse. In court, Dirk had accused me of stealing his medical records. Dirk told the judge that he had left his papers on the counter in our apartment, and I had stolen them to use against him. I did not take his medical records or even see them on moving day. I'm not sure if he thought accusing me of theft would help his case, or if he just lost his copy of those records. However, in his paranoia and disorganized thinking, Dirk had submitted his complete medical records, including his mental health records, as part of our divorce paperwork.

My lawyer called me overjoyed. He wanted me to come to his office right away. When I arrived, he shared that Dirk had submitted the results of his psychological evaluation: intense anger issues, sexual addiction, and mood problems. He smiled, "If there were room here, I'd do cartwheels!" His revelations strengthened our court case considerably.

Continuing the conversation on this brighter note, my lawyer asked if Dirk had ever threatened to kill himself or disappear. I said, "Yes."

My lawyer remarked, "Don't you hate it when they don't keep their promises?" I laughed. I couldn't believe he would say such a thing, but it was true. Dirk did not keep his word.

Before the next court appearance, Dirk had visited with Ally and been supervised by the pastor. He had given her a stuffed Scooby-Doo dog toy—the same one that a student had given me at Christmas when I taught at the Christian school in Hawaii. I knew Dirk's giving it to her was a message to me.

∞

Finally, after three months of living in danger, fear, and hiding, the judge granted my attorney's petition, in part, because of the diagnoses documented on Dirk's medical records. I was allowed to go back to South Carolina where I could renew my teaching certificate, and Ally and I could begin a new life.

I met with my lawyer, advocate, and counselor the next day. The situation was tense. Although I was allowed to leave, actually getting away was the most dangerous step. They shared statistics of women who were killed by their abuser as they tried to leave. I suddenly realized that leaving Seattle could be just as hazardous to my health as staying.

I carefully packed as many belongings as I could into the trunk of my car and shipped it to South Carolina. My parents planned to meet Ally and me at the airport. They would let me borrow a car until mine arrived two weeks later via the transport. I hired movers to ship my belongings from the secret storage unit to South Carolina. Chloe and I held a yard sale, getting rid of anything that wouldn't fit in the moving truck. I could not afford any excess charges.

As we reviewed the plan, I was even more heartbroken at the comprehension that I couldn't handle taking a baby, my two cats, our suitcases, stroller, and car seat on the plane. I simply couldn't do it all by myself.

Also, I couldn't afford to ship both of my cats. I was inconsolable, but I had to take them to the local shelter. As I read over the papers to surrender my dear pets, the shelter caretaker said they could take in the younger one but could not take the older cat. "No one will adopt him because of his age," he explained. "Your cat would be euthanized in a month to make space for younger cats."

I had already lost so much; I couldn't leave my precious cat there to die; he had been with me for almost twelve years. I paid $400 to ship my cat on a cargo flight to me in South Carolina. We would pick him up a few days after we had arrived.

I carefully planned one last supervised visit for Ally with Dirk. I dropped her off at the pastor's house and told the pastor this would be her last visit. I thanked him for his help, although I wasn't sure how much help he had been. I know he had been trying to follow the Lord about how to handle our relationship, but he surely didn't have all the facts.

After Ally visited with Dirk and the pastor's family, I took her back to Alice's house. I repacked our suitcases; we'd been living out of them for almost three months. Hopefully, this was the last time I would have to pack them again.

We had a last supper and family devotions with Alice and her family. In the end, we held hands in a circle as they prayed for our safety. They watched and waved us off as Alice's husband drove us to the hotel since we had shipped my car a few days before.

We spent the night in a hotel adjoining the airport. Immediately, I put out the Do Not Disturb sign and put a chair against the doorknob. Ally went to sleep in her playpen like most nights, but I was so scared! I didn't think Dirk knew where I was, but I wasn't taking any chances. I finally passed out in emotional exhaustion around 2:30 a.m. and slept a few hours.

We made it through airport security and found our seats on the plane without incident. Ally sat on my lap and napped most of the flight. For the first time in a while, I did not have to be on alert for another possible attack, so I was able to nap with her.

My parents met Ally and me at the airport. I was ready to make a new beginning for us. The first stop was our trailer and then to a picnic hosted by some friends of my brother who lived in the same town.

25. NEW BEGINNINGS

"To everything, there is a season and a time to every purpose under the heaven." - Ecclesiastes 3:1 KJV

My mother was reluctant to allow me to have my furniture and household items at their South Carolina home. I wondered if she believed some of Dirk's rants. She seemed unsure of my divorce and "virtual affair" situation, although I tried to assure her that I had not lost my mind and knew how to behave as a Christian woman.

Behind the scenes, my aunt, an amazingly strong woman who had survived her abusive husband, had helped encourage my mother to allow Ally and me to have our belongings in the house. My mom reluctantly agreed, but she had three strict rules for living in their home. First, no men were allowed as overnight guests. Secondly, I could not have loud or alcoholic parties. Lastly, I could not date for at least a year if I wanted to live in their second home.

I couldn't believe that, at thirty-something years old, my mother thought I would become involved in any of these activities. Didn't she know me at all? I was offended, but I had no other place to go, so I agreed to her conditions.

I unpacked our belongings and settled in our new home. Nothing was in my name for my safety. The house was in my parents' names. My cell phone was in my dad's name, and even our cable and utility bills were in my parents' names. Although we had taken these precautionary steps, I knew I was still in great danger.

Even though I was living across the country from Dirk, I was still having trouble sleeping. I expected him to be lurking around every corner. I regularly watched in my rearview mirror for Dirk's truck when I drove anywhere. I contacted the local police department as a domestic violence victim as part of the plan that Susan, my lawyer, and I had made. The police department directed me to their town's domestic violence advocate. Thankfully, she was able to help me get an alarm system installed. She suggested that I sign an order for the police to break down my door if the alarm were to go off without my calling in with the code word. I was following my safety plan.

Despite allowing me to leave the state, the judge in our divorce and custody case had ordered that Dirk be allowed to have video visits with Ally. It sickened me to have to set her up at my computer so Dirk could talk with her. I moved my laptop to the living room so that Ally could play while Dirk spoke with her.

As if he knew that I was standing slightly off screen, Dirk made snide remarks to me. "Tell your mommy she's raising you with no manners because you didn't say, "Yes, Sir." "Your mommy isn't as pretty as you," he would tell her.

Although Ally did not understand his comments, I recognized Dirk's skillful attempts to manipulate me like he used to. I was determined not to let him get to me. Although I would never admit it to him, the jabs hurt.

What happened to the loving marriage we had?

Continuing to follow my safety plan, I rented a post office box in a nearby town with a different zip code so Dirk could send gifts to Ally. I did not want him to have our address.

Dirk sent gifts that were quite disturbing to me and proved he hadn't given up trying to control me. He sent Ally stuffed animals and collectible Scooby-Doo toys that had belonged to me before our divorce. He sent her a book about the Ten Commandments with a note he had written inside the front cover, "Daddy prays that you keep these better than your mommy." Another gift box included a squirrel skin because he "knew she would like it because it is soft." It was creepy and inappropriate for a young child.

Since the pastor was still in Washington State and, thus, unable to supervise visits, I had to agree to someone else to monitor in-person visits between Dirk and Ally. He was still allowed to see Ally in person if he traveled to South Carolina to do so. I decided to let Dirk's mom and stepfather manage Ally's in-person visits with him. Dirk's mother had remarried and started a very successful business with her husband. They were threatening to sue me for grandparents' visitation rights. I couldn't afford another court battle; I didn't even have a job at this point. I felt backed into a corner, and I didn't dare say no. Besides, Dirk's stepfather was a retired law enforcement officer. Surely he would keep "Papa's Princess," as he called her, safe and would follow all the rules.

At thanksgiving, Dirk, his mom, and step-father drove to South Carolina to pick up Ally, drive her to their home in Florida for a week, and then planned to bring her back to me. When she came back, I was amazed at the bags of new designer-label clothes and toys she had packed with her things. She had picked out seventeen new outfits. She and her nana had gone shopping. One outfit even had a matching hat, purse, and shoes because granny said all girls love shoes.

After a spring visit, despite the designer clothes and accessories, I could tell something was off. They had taken her to have Easter pictures made with a real bunny. She was wearing a white Ralph Lauren dress with a black satin belt, matching hat, gloves, socks, and black patent leather shoes. "And don't forget the purse, Momma," she said when I told her the outfit was beautiful. I loved the pictures.

However, after seeing her grandparents during that visit, Ally was so upset. She was crying and just wanted to sit on my lap to hug me. His mother had shared that there was an incident when Dirk ridiculed Ally for not being able to reach the bathroom light switch, and He wouldn't let her out until she used the toilet. Ally was scared of the dark and had an accident. When we got home, she wouldn't let me out of her sight. Ally cried when I closed the door to the bathroom to give me privacy on the toilet.

I was angry. Dirk was hurting my little girl, and I couldn't protect her. The judge had ruled. I was powerless. I felt that all I could do was to mitigate the damage.

During this time, Ally began sleepwalking. Subconsciously, she was calling me and coming to find me. In her night terrors, she would clearly describe her fears. It always included her seeing a man hurting a little girl. I picked her up, hugged her close, and took her back to her room. I tucked her back in with her favorite stuffed dog, Flower, under her arm. I kissed her goodnight and said a silent prayer that God would keep us safe and would comfort her. I made sure to leave the hall light on in case she got up again. I didn't know what to do. I went to a local attorney, but he would not take my case. I didn't have any money, and I had no proof of Dirk's recent abuse. Ally's nightmares were not enough to prove anything in court.

Besides all the trauma of visitation, Dirk continued to run up our joint credit cards. He had always been terrible with his money, spending it all without thought of paying bills or buying food. Although we were separated, we still had to pay off our joint credit cards. I vividly remembered Dirk threatening to buy a Cadillac, in both of our names, and to make me pay for it. He said that he would make me pay because my parents could afford it, and they would always take care of Ally and me. Now it seemed that he was still charging items to the credit card that I was assigned to pay off as part of our court settlement.

The judge ordered Dirk to pay alimony and child support. I tried to deposit the money at my bank, but several of his checks bounced. So, each month Ally and I trekked to a branch of Dirk's bank to cash it, or at least to see if there was money to pay it.

On a happy note, Carlee lived a short drive from my parents' home in South Carolina. It was great to have a friend nearby. Ally and I spent a lot of time with Carlee and her family. Carlee's parents had come to live with them since they couldn't take care of themselves any longer.

Carlee, her mother, and I spent hours talking, laughing, and healing. God had put them in the right place at the right time for Ally and me. Carlee's mom became "Nana," and we became what they called "Calabash family." Even Carlee's sisters welcomed us with open arms.

Over dinner with Carlee's family, I mentioned my financial difficulties and calls from Dirk's debt collectors. The next day Carlee's husband, a Navy Command Master Chief, called Dirk's command to inform them of his debts, his failure to pay his bills, and the bounced child support checks. I didn't even know that had been an option. Somehow Dirk found out that it was Carlee's husband who had reported his activities, and Dirk threatened to press charges for harassment. But at least Dirk stopped charging his purchases to my card, and his command knew about his financial troubles. They ordered him to pay and garnished his wages for the court-ordered child support.

Would I ever get away from him and his threats? I felt hopeless.

Even people who were brave enough to help me were harassed and threatened. Anyone I reached out to ask for help put themselves in danger. Would it ever end?

26. FINALIZATION

"I will place on his shoulder the key to the house of David; what he opens no one can shut, and what he shuts no one can open."
— Isaiah 22:22 NIV

After the ninety-day waiting period decreed by Washington, the court finalized my divorce. I was relieved to end that chapter of my life, at least on paper. I was not free of the debts; I still had to pay them, but I was no longer bound to Dirk.

Carlee and Nana suggested that we have a celebration. The kids loved the Chuck E. Cheese restaurant, so we had the party there. Nana declared, "Publix cakes are the best; they fit every situation." She ordered a cake with "Congratulations on Your Divorce" written on it! We shared a good laugh about how a cake could fit every situation—even finalizing a divorce. The kids couldn't read the words anyway. They wanted to eat all the delicious extra frosting on the edges.

The next week, while cooking dinner for myself and Ally, I realized that I could have squash for dinner, and no one would be upset with me. I could add onions to my food. I could eat whatever I wanted without negative consequences.

What do I like? It had been so long since I had thought about me. *What was my favorite color? What did I want to wear? Am I allowed to make these decisions?*

In a phone conversation with my mother, she commented, "You have changed. I don't know you anymore."

"Mom, I realized I needed to reevaluate my life. Somehow,

when my face hit the glass, my perspective changed."

I had done everything a good Christian girl should do. I was following all the dos and don'ts of my church. I had an excellent Christian pedigree. Besides being a descendent of pastors and Bible teachers, I attended Christian school from first through twelfth grades and then a well-known Christian university. I went on three summer mission trips and worked as a Christian school teacher on the mission field in Hawaii. I had saved myself for marriage and submitted to my husband with a glad heart. I had prayed for my marriage and been faithful, even as Dirk broke my heart. I had volunteered at church, attended faithfully, and ministered about God's good news to everyone I met. I thought I knew God, but that all changed the day my face hit the glass of the storm door in my apartment.

In that instant, all that I had thought was important wasn't! All the rules I'd followed and relied on as proof that I was a good Christian—wearing dresses or shorts down to my knees, wearing earrings no larger than a dime, not attending R-rated movies, and so forth—didn't matter. God wouldn't love me more because I followed those rules. Keeping them hadn't kept me safe or made my marriage work. These rules were insignificant compared with my reality of being stalked, homeless, and caring for my baby girl alone. I realized that following those rules would never determine my eternal future. "For by grace are ye saved, through faith; and not of yourselves; it is the gift of God: Not of works, lest any man should boast," (Ephesians 2:8-9 KJV).

In the relative safety of my new home in South Carolina, I had time to think through and process my beliefs. I didn't like the way I had come to this place, bruised, defeated, and scared. I wouldn't wish this terrible situation for anyone. I wanted to trust that God would help me through this situation, but, how would He?

I was now divorced, jobless, and a newly-single parent. Would God help me even here?

27. MEETING JOSH

"For I know the thoughts that I think toward you," saith the Lord, "thoughts of peace, and not of evil, to give you an expected end." – Jeremiah 29:11 KJV

I had to find a job quickly. Since I was living in my parents' house, I wouldn't be homeless or starve, but clothing, car insurance, and gas? Those required a steady income.

Dirk had left me just enough money to disqualify me from any type of government assistance: no food stamps, child care money, or subsidized health care. I couldn't tell if this was a blessing or yet another way of tormenting me.

While searching online for local help wanted, I found an ad for a job teaching at a Christian School at a nearby church. The announcement mentioned elementary school, but I had taught both first and sixth grades before, and I had a Christian School teaching certificate. I considered myself qualified.

I went to the interview and was offered the job on the spot. Christian school teachers don't come along very often. However, what I thought would be teaching elementary school was actually teaching four-year-old kindergarteners. Because I needed the job, I agreed, even though it wouldn't have been my first choice.

I still felt as if I were in hiding, so I only left the safety of my South Carolina home to go to work and Carlee's house. Ally attended the church daycare where I worked. I taught in the four-year-old room, telling Bible stories, math, reading, supervising playtime, making crafts, and putting them down for naptime.

The church board-appointed daycare director made sure I only worked 30 – 35 hours a week, with the result that the church and school did not have to offer health care or other benefits as I was considered a part-time worker. The other ladies who worked at the daycare were close friends and extended family of the director. I was an outsider, not only because I was recently divorced, but also because I was a "Yankee" from the north.

One morning, through my closed classroom door, I heard the other ladies talking in the hallway. I opened my door to see what was going on. It was someone's birthday, so they had all ordered from a local restaurant. I had been excluded. When I asked Shannon, the five-year-olds' teacher in the classroom next to mine, why I wasn't included, she said, "We don't know you! We didn't think you'd want to join us." Her nasty comments continued as she added, "And besides, you and your daughter are Yankees. You're *not* welcome here!"

Some days later, one of the boys had a bathroom accident. Making the situation worse by trying to clean it up, he had created an enormous mess in our small classroom water closet. As I called for someone to help me, Shannon declared, "Ain't no one gonna help you with that." The other ladies were busy when I needed to use the restroom, so I had to wait for someone to watch the children in my class or use their little water closet. I couldn't bring myself to use the tiny preschool-sized toilet. I had to wait. It seemed I was on my own, even working in a church daycare, where I thought everyone should have been welcomed and included.

When I wasn't at work, I spent all of my time with Ally. We had settled in at my parents' place. It had been over a year, and I felt safer than I had in a while. After school, Ally and I would go home to play, and then I made supper. After more playtime or a cartoon binge, we would pick up the toys and get ready for bed.

Every night I would tuck her in with a story and Bible song. We would pray together to thank God for two good things that happened to us that day and say goodnight. I'd pick up the few toys she left out in the living room, put them in the corner basket, make myself a cup of tea and go to my bedroom.

The evenings were mostly quiet, but I was still on edge, feeling nervous and afraid as if Dirk would come for us at any time. Be that as it may, I forced myself to focus on and remember the talks with Susan. She suggested I make a gratitude journal, writing down at least two happy items that happened each day. Simple everyday incidents like getting a shower without Ally crying because she couldn't see me, paydays, or even that the sun was shining, and God had given us another day became journal entries. Noting things that I was grateful for helped me focus on the positive in the middle of all the continuing emotional upheaval.

I worked for a year at that church daycare. When the regular school term ended in June, I quit. Meanwhile, my mom was concerned about my lack of income; I didn't have a career to support myself and my daughter. I didn't know what I was going to do. Maybe I would work at a fast food place, but it couldn't be as bad as the way those church daycare ladies treated me, being ignored and shunned every single day. I needed a different job.

On a hot July afternoon, I popped in to see my sister-in-law, Katherine, and my nieces. They lived in a housing development a few minutes away from my parent's trailer where Ally and I lived. She was working at her wheel, making pots and other ceramic pieces to sell at her booth in the downtown craft barn as we chatted about my job situation. The local middle school where my nieces attended had recently earned a blue ribbon national award. She knew they were looking for a computer teacher, and I happened to be one. I told her that I had applied but hadn't heard back from them. Everyone knew everyone in our small town, and I was a newcomer.

She had a plan. She knew the head secretary, Helen, loved her floral-scented organic soy candles in the handmade ceramic holders, so she decided that she would take one to her and I should happen to go with her to meet Helen in person. Then, as part of the polite conversation, we would mention that I had sent in a teacher application and inquire about the status.

Her plan worked perfectly! Helen loved the candle, and I got an interview and offered the job. The principal loved my nieces since they were model students, and my brother was a volunteer girls softball coach whom the kids all loved. I was in! I would begin teaching keyboarding and computer literacy in August. The school was less than ten minutes from my house, and Ally could go to a different church preschool nearby. I was thrilled. I would have a steady paycheck with health insurance and even a retirement plan. God had provided a much better place for us.

Unfortunately, I could not prevent Dirk from continuing his court-ordered video visits with Ally. I stayed close, but always out of his view. Hearing the sound of his voice made me feel nauseated. When I knew he and his parents were coming to see Ally, I would vomit every time. I'm sure it was nerves, but being sick to my stomach, along with my fear of seeing Dirk, was dreadful.

The state of Washington had finally convinced the Navy payroll office to garnish Dirk's paycheck, so we didn't have to go to the bank or worry about his checks bouncing. The money was directly deposited into my account. I was relieved to have that money coming in, even if my alimony would only last one year. I wanted to get back on my feet and cut all ties with Dirk.

The Navy transferred Dirk to San Diego, California. I was relieved that he was farther away, but he continued his video visits with Ally. She liked seeing him at first, but he wanted her to sit in front of the screen and just talk or watch him. I don't think he realized that preschoolers don't just sit quietly and talk like he expected of her.

Each evening after Ally went to bed, I would read different devotional and fun books, watch television, or play my silly computer game. My new counselor called the computer game an escape, a coping mechanism, and she thought it was great for me to keep playing. She said it was healthy for me to have some time when I wasn't focused on the danger we could be in all the time.

In the online game, we used an internet-based communication system, like a video conference call, to help our group coordinate characters, positions, resources, and teamwork. All these things were critical to the success of our twenty-five-person mission of slaying the evil dragon. One night, out of the blue, one of the other players told me that I could play my role better if I would follow his instructions. I didn't know him, and I was taken aback by his know-it-all attitude. Who was he to tell me what to do?

Playing the same game a few days later, Rick, someone I knew from my game group, introduced me to that same guy, Josh. Over the game communication system, Josh apologized for giving the impression of being a know-it-all. However, he had written several articles and guides on playing the type of character I played. Thus, he did know quite a bit; I was surprised. Continuing the conversation, Rick, Josh, and I laughed as we told stories of the strange dates we had been on and the trials of being single with married friends.

I shared that, after taking the year my mother suggested, my friends had arranged for me to go on several blind dates. One man told me that since he had paid for dinner, I was obligated to sleep with him. I politely disagreed and left. Another man excused himself from the table at the restaurant to use the men's restroom. Less than two minutes later, he texted me from the bathroom saying that he was "having a good time." I had finished dinner, so I left. As I drove out of the parking lot headed home, he texted at least eight more times. It was only a ten-minute drive. Annoyed, when I arrived home I texted back that I didn't want to hear from him again. When Josh shared how one of his dates complained that "global warming was ruining her tan," I couldn't keep myself from laughing out loud.

Toward the end of our conversation, Josh suggested that he needed to take me on a traditional date. He wanted to show me there were still decent men in the world. "I need to redeem the reputation of the males in the world," he said.

We traded phone numbers, and Josh called me. I was amazed by how easy he was to talk to. We began talking almost daily—for several hours. We talked about everything from politics to current events and personal issues to Christianity and the Bible. I relished our talks. We were becoming close friends.

During one conversation, Josh reminded me that he had asked me on a date. "It will never happen," I said teasingly. I knew he would never come to South Carolina, and I wasn't going to New England.

"What would convince you of my intentions?"

"A plane ticket itinerary and a hotel reservation," I answered flippantly.

Josh said, "Give me 30 minutes."

Not even twenty minutes later, Josh's flight itinerary and hotel reservation appeared in my email box.

He's serious. Wow!

I made plans with my sister-in-law, Katherine, for Ally to spend the weekend with her and my nieces. I didn't want her to meet Josh in case things were not as they seemed.

Josh flew to the nearest airport to my home on Columbus Day weekend. I met him at his hotel for dinner. Despite all my misgivings as to how the evening would turn out, the natural conversations we had on the phone continued and were even better in person. We moved from the restaurant to comfortable seats in the atrium area, surrounded by the meticulously arranged plants and water fountains. We talked, laughed, and enjoyed each other's company until the early morning hours. When I finally realized the time, I said I needed to go home to sleep. We made plans to go sightseeing in the morning since he had never been to South Carolina. We hugged good night, and he kissed my cheek. I was impressed by his thoughtfulness

In the morning, I went to my brother's house to check on Ally. As I popped my head in the door, Ally spied me and said, "Hi, Momma, I'm playing," and after that she turned around to go back to her toys. Assured that she was having fun and didn't need me, I thanked Katherine for helping out and left.

I met Josh in the lobby of his hotel to show him around my town and to see all the tourist sites. We enjoyed another fantastic day of laughing, talking, and getting to know one another. As the weekend ended, we agreed to meet in person more often to see where our relationship would go.

We had been talking two to three hours daily for several months when Josh asked, "Have you and Ally ever been to Disney World?" I explained that we had been there once about a year before and Ally loved it. Chip and Dale were the first characters she hugged and had had her picture taken with them, but her favorite Disney characters were the 101 Dalmatians.

Josh's job required him to travel quite a bit, so he related how he stacked hotel points and flight miles. He had amassed enough to take us to Disney World for four days. Did we want to go with him? Yes! That sounded like great fun. I was floored that he would treat us to such a fantastic trip. Ally liked Josh; she had met him when we dropped him off at the airport that Columbus Day weekend. He had it all planned out. He booked us a suite at the DoubleTree Hotel so that Ally and I could share one room, and he would have the other. Besides, the DoubleTree had a Disney bus service so that we could ride the bus to the parks. Josh had everything all planned out. I couldn't believe how thoughtful he was and how he wanted to take such good care of us.

Josh flew to South Carolina, where Ally and I met him at the airport. He asked to stop at Sonic, mentioning that it was one of his favorite fast-food restaurants, and there was no Sonic within driving distance of his New England condo. Ally and I liked Sonic, too. After stopping for cherry limeade, diet cherry Dr. Pepper, and blue ocean water drinks and tater tots, we headed to our house. Ally and I finally considered it ours since we had been living there for almost three years at this point. We needed to pick up our things and travel to Orlando.

I remember Josh's reaction vividly as we walked in the door. "This is a big pile of stuff!" he exclaimed. I laughed. There were two suitcases, one each for Ally and me, Ally's blankets, her unicorn pillow pet and stuffed animals, her car bag with things to do while driving, snacks, drinks, and all the things that would make two ladies happy while traveling.

We loaded up the car and drove about eight hours to Orlando, arriving in time for a late dinner and a swim. As I sat on the edge of the pool, I watched Ally ask Josh if she could jump into the water. "Catch me!" she yelled happily. My heart melted as I noticed Josh's giant grin and how he hugged Ally as she jumped into his waiting arms. Ally deserved a man in her life who would always catch her, and I was realizing, I did too.

After a while in the chilly pool water, Josh and I went to the hot tub. The warm water felt great after sitting in the car and traveling all day; however, seeing us sitting in the warm water gave

Ally an idea. She would make us into soup, similar to the way she had seen grandpa cook up a homemade soup. As Josh and I soaked in the warmth, Ally walked around the outside of the hot tub while pretending to throw in vegetables like carrots, celery, and peas, although she would not eat them, and some "other stuff" she mentioned. Then she instructed us to move in a circle so that we could help her stir her soup. We played along with her until she started yawning. We dried off and went up to our room to sleep. We could hardly wait for the morning.

We got up bright and early the next day. After getting off the Disney bus to the park, we walked to the entrance. Ally looked up at Josh and asked, "My feet are tired. Carry me?" She was using the smile that I knew got her almost everything she wanted. He returned her smile and boosted her up onto his shoulders. "Yeah!" she exclaimed. It seemed the two of them were hitting it off. I was captivated watching them interact.

The pinnacle moment came when Josh said he was thirsty for some frozen lemonade. Josh had picked up two straws for the lemonade in case Ally or I wanted some. I drank water, but Ally wanted to taste Josh's drink. I think her favorite foods were anything that was on anyone else's plate but hers. Laughingly, we called it the "Ally diet," since we didn't have to worry about finishing all the food on our plates, saving us from all the calories.

She liked Josh's frozen lemonade so well that she drank almost all of it. I snapped one of my most favorite pictures as Ally and Josh drank the lemonade from their separate straws at the same time. We rode the different rides, ate breakfast with Winnie the Pooh, and overall had an unbelievably delightful time. I hadn't had that much fun in years. Josh teased me as he watched Ally and I dance to the music of the afternoon parade in the Magic Kingdom. I was feeling safe, able to relax, trust Josh with Ally, and happier than I had been in a long, long time. I felt wonderful.

Later Josh mentioned that when he disclosed his plans to his dad, his Pops had told him, "You don't take a woman and her child to Disney World if you aren't serious about them." Josh wasn't sure what he meant, but the statement made me think about our relationship. Was Pops right? Was there something deeper here? Josh had stood in the queue to see Tinkerbell and the fairies with us for almost two hours. Thinking about that made my heart flutter like I imagined the fairy wings fluttering, but I was not sure I was ready for a serious commitment yet. I was only beginning to heal.

28. NEW POSSIBILITIES

"Behold, I will do a new thing; now it shall spring forth; shall ye not know it? I will even make a way in the wilderness and rivers in the desert."
—Isaiah 43: 19 KJV

Ally and I had lived in South Carolina for almost four years. We still lived in my parents' house, although we considered it ours. Ally loved her new preschool, and I did, too. In her four-year-old kindergarten class, Ally learned to read. She loved to read everything she could get her hands on. One morning on our way to school, she was reading all the store and street signs as I was listening to the local talk radio station.

The radio station was discussing politics and "the issues" of the moment when I heard from the back seat, "Momma, what are the issues?" I smiled, "The issues are what people think is important in the election that's coming up." I told her about the police, taxes, and unemployment, people who didn't have jobs. She sweetly replied, "Oh, those issues are important." I agreed. I don't think I could have put it better myself. I hugged her goodbye as I dropped her off at pre-school. She waved and turned excitedly as she joined her friends. I drove back to the middle school to teach my computer students.

Josh and I continued talking for hours almost daily, and he came to see Ally and me as often as he could. We had discussed my past in depth. He was heartbroken that anyone could treat Ally and me so horribly. Trusting Josh with my deepest secrets, I disclosed some of my emotional baggage around being abused. I startle easily. Ally and I don't do surprises. We have schedules and lists; we plan and organize our life. Chaos upsets us by bringing back painful memories. As Josh and I discussed my past abuse, I wanted him to be aware of what he was getting into as we were getting serious. I opened myself up to him. I was vulnerable, and he was gentle and kind with my heart.

We dated for several years. Josh would come for all the critical events in our lives. He arrived at Halloween so that he could carve Ally's pumpkin. Josh visited at Easter and for Ally's kindergarten graduation. He was becoming an integral part of our family, and I couldn't imagine my life without him anymore.

After Ally's kindergarten graduation, we planned another trip to Disney. I was thrilled. I was going to one of my favorite places with my favorite people! When Ally and I picked up Josh from the airport, he asked to stop at Walmart. He had forgotten his socks and toothbrush. Josh frequently traveled for his job, so I regarded him forgetting anything as very unusual. I had never seen him in disarray. Of course, we stopped; he needed those items for our trip.

That evening Josh grilled pork chops outside, and I made the salad for dinner. Ally wanted chicken nuggets, rice, and green beans—her favorite everyday meal. After dinner, we played with her and watched her favorite movie again. She went to bed after our usual hugs, kisses, bedtime prayers, and me singing to her. She invited Josh to come in to pray with us.

Once Ally was asleep, Josh called me outside to sit on the back porch to savor the warm, fall Carolina evening. Josh looked down and inexplicably apologized for what he was about to do. He seemed nervous and unsteady. I was perplexed by his apology.

I looked at him in bewilderment as he knelt at the bottom of the porch steps. He reached into his pocket and retrieved a small jewelry box. Opening it, he held out one of the most massive diamond rings I had ever seen. His hands and his voice were shaking, and I thought I saw tears in his eyes.

"Will you marry me?"

"YES!" With happy tears, I hugged him.

I couldn't believe that I had found someone whom I could

trust enough to fall asleep with his arm around my shoulders as we watched television in the evenings. This was a Christian man who loved me unconditionally, despite all my scars, emotional baggage and all--Josh loved me. He was candid enough to admit that he didn't understand all that I had been through, but he could promise to stand beside me and hold my hand as we dealt with all of it together. He loved me. God was good!

As we went back into the house, he revealed that he had planned to propose to me with Ally in front of Cinderella's castle; but he was nervous and didn't want to wait until we got there. I didn't mind. Going to Walt Disney World would be our engagement trip.

I wanted him to ask my parents for their blessing, so our first call was to them. They said Josh's proposal was not unexpected, and they gave their consent. We planned to be married the following June.

Josh had already told Pops, who gave an "I told you so" speech, but said he couldn't wait to meet us. He thought Ally and I must be special to capture Josh's heart so completely. The thought warmed my own heart. It still felt surreal that someone like Josh—someone caring, gentle, kind, and strong—loved me that much.

The next morning Ally woke up Josh, who was sleeping on the couch. "I want to watch PBS Kids," she announced.

"Ally, I have something important to ask you," Josh said as he patted the couch next to him. When she climbed up and snuggled next to him, he said, "Ally, I want to marry your mom. Would you let me?"

Ally looked at him with a frown, shaking her head. "No." Off she went, from the couch to her room to play. She had given her final word.

Josh couldn't believe her answer and neither could I. He followed her to her room to ask why. He knocked gently and asked if he could come into her room to talk with her. At her direction, he took a seat at her tiny wooden table. Ally had prepared a tea party setting out her dishes, pretend tea, and cookies, of course. They talked over their delicious tea. Ally's reasoning was sweet. "If you marry Mommy, I will have to share you with her."

Josh smiled. "Well, if I marry your mommy, I will get to live with you, and I'll see you all the time."

Ally seemed pleased with that idea. She thought for a moment and finally said, "Ok, you can marry *us*."

During our engagement, Josh came to spend Christmas with us in South Carolina. My dad had asked Josh what he wanted when he would arrive after the thirteen-hour drive to our home. Josh joked, "A cherry pie would be great." I had discovered that my dad's favorite pie was also Josh's favorite. When Josh arrived, he was greeted by a pot of hot coffee and a homemade, freshly baked cherry pie that was warming on the stove.

We had a wonderful Christmas. In the family tradition, we attended the Christmas Eve service at church. After we got home and Ally had changed into her pajamas, we got to open one gift and eat the Christmas cookies that Ally, Grandma, and I had baked and decorated, another happy family tradition.

Ally and I prepared a plate of cookies and a mug of hot chocolate for Santa. She told me what to write in his letter that we left next to the cookies. We also set out a bowl of oats and a few carrots for Santa's reindeer. We didn't want them to be hungry on their long journey.

After hugs, kisses, bedtime prayers, and Mommy singing to her, Ally went to sleep. The "elves"—Grandpa Elf and Josh Elf—went out to the shed to assemble Ally's new bike. When it was constructed and placed next to the Christmas tree, we all had tea and coffee, and then we went to our separate bedrooms.

The next morning, Josh and I snuggled together on the couch as we watched Ally tear open her presents. Watching her was such a joy. I looked from Ally to Josh with hope burning brightly in my heart—hope that we could have a happy life together as a family. Most of all, this time I had faith that I had found a love that would last.

I'll Pray for You

29. SECOND CHANCES

"Now unto him, that is able to do exceedingly abundantly above all that we ask or think, according to the power that worketh in us, 21Unto him be glory in the church by Christ Jesus throughout all ages, world without end. Amen." — Ephesians 3:20-21 KJV

After being engaged for a year, Josh and I were married in a small ceremony in June. Josh's best friends, Ken and Rick, came to be part of the festivities, along with Carlee and her kids. Our families were thrilled to meet each other and share our joy.

We decorated for the ceremony the night before. We placed a single stem of blue orchids in a clear glass vase on each table, along with royal blue napkins, some confetti, and a disposable camera for guests to take candid shots. Josh, Ken, and Rick built a gazebo as a backdrop where we would stand to recite our vows. My mom and Ally wrapped the gauzy material for decorating the gazebo around their necks as if they were wearing feather boas with arms outspread. Ally called, "Ta da, we look fabulous, darling." Laughing, I snapped the picture.

Josh and Ken practiced where Josh and I would stand in order to center the gazebo. Ken smiled at me and joked, "He was mine first, and don't you forget it." Laughter and fun filled the air, unlike my first wedding.

Was this the way marriage, a relationship, a family, should be? There was so much joy, laughter, and even jokes and silliness. My heart was full. Had God given Ally and me a second chance to be happy? *Was this what God had in mind for me--something better with which to bless me?*

30. NEW LIFE

"But Jesus beheld them, and said unto them, with men, this is impossible; but with God, all things are possible."
— Matthew 19:26 KJV

After the wedding, Josh, Ken, and Rick helped pack our things into the moving truck to head to New England to live with Josh. Ally, who thought every stranger was just a friend she had not yet met, loved Ken and Rick instantly. Rick and his wife were fun, in her opinion, but Uncle Ken, as she called him, was the best! Uncle Ken had brought his girlfriend, Desiree. They were getting serious, and he wanted her to meet Josh, Ally, and me. As Josh and I were mingling and taking pictures at the reception, Ally voiced her thoughts to Ken. "Desiree's nice; you should marry her." He told Ally he was "working on it." About two years later, we attended their wedding. Ally was right.

We sent our belongings in the moving truck but, as we had foreseen, Josh received an urgent work assignment requiring him to fly to Hawaii, and I joined him there to kick off our honeymoon. I met him in Honolulu and showed him some of my favorite places from when I had lived there. We made happy memories to replace the dark ones. I felt my heart getting lighter with every smile and laugh. It was nice to be back in Hawaii and to feel like it was mine again.

When Josh's meetings concluded, we flew to Fiji and checked into a Hilton resort on Denarau Island. Our honeymoon was fabulous. We sat on the *lanai* of our condo and watched the ocean waves. We talked about our dreams, our wedding, and the gorgeous tropical resort. One of the resort staff climbed a coconut tree and threw us down fresh coconuts because he wanted us to try the coconut water straight out of the fruit. It tasted nutty and refreshing. Another day he brought us fresh oranges from the tree in his yard.

I had brought a couples' devotion book we received as a wedding gift. As we sat on the *lanai*, Josh drinking coffee and me with tea, looking out at God's creation, I read the Bible passage and the short devotion. Then we prayed together. I felt as if I were on top of the world. Josh loved Ally and me. We were here in an amazingly gorgeous country for our honeymoon, and we could pray and discuss God and His Word. God had given me more than I ever dreamed was possible.

To top off a fantastic honeymoon, Josh and I were bumped into first class for our flight back to New England. I accepted this as another generous blessing from God.

31. SCARS

*"Beware of false prophets, which come to you in sheep's clothing, but
inwardly they are ravening wolves." – Matthew 7:15 KJV*

Life in New England took some getting used to but, eventually,
we settled in and found friends. I got a job teaching computer
technology at a local, public middle school. Everyone I work with
is professional and respectful and would never consider my past
as a reason to fire me. They lift me up, support me, and allow me
to be fully myself, even at my messiest.

As a rule, public schools do not allow any type of religious
teachings unless the students ask. However, our school district
declares Rosh Hashanah and Yom Kippur as "no school" holidays
since a large population of practicing Jews lives in that area. When
some students ask what those mean, I am allowed to share the
Bible stories. Good Friday is a state holiday here in Rhode Island.
Considering that some students do not know the resurrection
story, they ask, "Why is that Friday considered good?" In
answering their questions, I share the gospel in the Easter story
from the Bible.

We found a church that Josh, Ally, and I all liked. The pastor
came to visit us and welcome us to town. As we talked, he asked
about our backgrounds. I shared candidly about my situation. The
pastor wept as he listened to a short version of our story.

I could not believe the pastor's next words, "I'm sorry. I'm so
sorry, Jesus loves you, but sometimes His children don't act so

loving." His words brought tears to my eyes. Convinced that God had better things ahead for our family, my past was in the past, he reassured me. It was one of the first times I felt safe enough with a pastor to let my guard down and to be honest about my recent experiences with church people.

Josh got the tissue box for the pastor and me. The pastor assured us that we would be welcome at the church anytime. He asked if he could hug me, and then he prayed with us. It had been a long time since I felt I would be welcome at a church.

I am still working through my scars and emotional baggage. I grapple with the realization that my life will never be the same. Dirk had threatened to destroy my life if I left him, and he did everything in his power to do that. However, he was not the only one with a part in destroying my past life. The churches and Christian schools in which I enjoyed serving God would no longer allow me to work there. Even though I know Jesus said, "Bear ye one another's burdens, and so fulfill the law of Christ," (Galatians 6:2 KJV). No exceptions in the "divorce and remarriage policy" are made. I can never go back. I am not welcome; I spent my whole life in this church denomination. The loss of the traditions and spiritual home and family still cuts me to the core sometimes. Jesus would not support the way I was treated.

I battle with all I have lost. Years of my life are dead. Gone! My former Christian friends, my career teaching in a Christian school, and my entire past life all vanished the instant my face hit the storm door.

At times I selfishly wish I could go back to that church elder on his back porch to tell him I survived, and, even without his help, God is still blessing me. I wish I could show him that, while he chose to abandon me to my fate in the hands of an abusive, wicked man, God never did.

God brought people into my life who saw me, helped me despite the significant risk to themselves, and gave me hope and friendship. It wasn't my church pastors, church elders, or devout Christian friends who treated me as Christ would have. No, it was navy wives filled with empathy and compassion, Alice and her family who were barely tolerated at our church, and the counselors and advocates who have found, at least to my mind, divine purpose in helping others.

God has given me a new life. It's different, but it's excellent! I have a new, more profound relationship with Him. No longer measuring my spirituality in a list of dos and don'ts, I have given up trying to appear to be the perfect Christian woman with an ideal family. I don't always attend every church service as I did before. I don't throw myself into church activities, as though church attendance alone would get me into heaven.

I now have a bond with God, my Heavenly Father, out of gratefulness for His love for me. When my life was in shambles, living in fear, without a home of my own, God was always there. He gave me His strength to stand up for myself, to escape from Dirk and his toxic abuse, and the power to build a new life for myself that He has blessed in abundance.

God has given me grace and mercy beyond all I could have dreamed. He keeps Ally and me safe daily, and I am grateful. My daughter is now a teenager with all the angst and questions about God and the world around us. Our life is messy and complicated; I have no more need to hide that. We are who God made us. God allows me to "Cast thy burden upon the Lord, and he shall sustain thee: he shall never suffer the righteous to be moved," (Psalm 55:22 KJV). God isn't interested in my being perfect. He wants us to be authentic, real, and open to Him in all things.

Sometimes all I can do is fall on my knees by the side of my bed at the end of the day and say, "Lord, you know all things, and you know my heart." I pour out my feelings to Him without pretense or an audience. "God, you are the only one who can" has become a routine sentence in my prayers. My faith is deeply personal, more than merely doing my duty.

I wish I could say that I am fully healed from my first marriage, but my scars will always remain. Random situations can trigger those old, fearful feelings. When a student slams his locker or someone comes up behind me quickly, I am startled. I jump. I tell my students I need a lot of personal space. Crowded or tight spaces bother me; I need to know where the exits are--all the time. We don't do surprises or jump scares at our house. Unexpected loud noises or shouting disturb my daughter and me.

A few weeks ago, Josh and I were cooking together in the kitchen. We like to make our tomato sauce from scratch for canning. As I was at the sink washing dishes, I didn't notice Josh walk up behind me. He hit the wooden spoon he was using on the side of the sink with a loud *thunk!*

I jumped and then hurried by him, running to the bathroom as an escape. I locked the door in a panic! Tears poured down my face, and my heart was pounding. I took some deep breaths; I heard Josh outside the door knocking gently.

"Are you ok?" he asked.

"I think so," I replied, wiping my tears and sniffling nose. "You scared me," I said between sobs.

"I'm so sorry." I could hear the raw emotion in his voice.

"I need a few minutes," I said, honestly knowing I needed to breathe and reassure myself that I was still safe.

"Okay, whenever you're ready." I heard him walk away.

Behind that locked bathroom door, I forced my mind to work through the raw emotions, the fear instinct that had taken over. Although I know, beyond any doubt, that Josh would never hurt me, those old feelings, the scars and emotional baggage, were still there. I don't think they will ever completely go away.

After praying and pulling myself together, I left the bathroom to find Josh. He was in the kitchen, stirring the sauce. He heard me approach and turned toward me. Both of us had tears in our eyes as I hugged him.

"*I'm sorry*," Josh whispered as he held me close, kissing the top of my head in a loving gesture of comfort. He was at a loss, not knowing what to do.

"*I'm sorry I reacted like that,*" I sniffled.

We held hands as we walked to the living room couch to talk and plan how to handle future "incidents."

I wish I could say there won't be any more instances similar to that one, but there could be. God allows time to heal our hurts, but the scars remain. My life will never be the same.

∞

God is not responsible for the actions, or inactions, of His followers. He loves me, with all my flaws, insecurities, and the emotional baggage of my abuse. I struggle with attending church regularly since God's people are not always understanding or merciful. Thankfully, church attendance or membership is no longer the basis for my relationship with my Heavenly Father. "Verily, verily, I say unto you, He that heareth my word, and believeth on him that sent me, hath everlasting life, and shall not come into condemnation; but is passed from death unto life," (John 5:24 KJV).

I am ashamed when I think back on the times that I was judgmental or less than merciful to someone who didn't fit my standards for a good, Christian woman. I wish I could take back every moment that I judged without knowing the whole story.

A "scarlet letter" seems to appear on my chest when we visit a church. When we attend long enough that I feel comfortable, I volunteer for a church ministry, as in my past life. Nonetheless, I am told, "no, thank you," but Josh is allowed to help since he was not married before God brought him to Ally and me.

We don't usually stay for the fellowship hour; people ask questions to which they don't want an honest answer. "Where are you from?" "What brings you to our town?" "Your daughter doesn't have the same last name as you and your husband?" Considering that people are alarmed at the answers, I either dodge the questions or avoid the situation.

I carry the shame of being divorced. I know deep in my heart that God's grace has forgiven my part in all of that. He has given me a life and love better than I ever imagined. Although I know Dirk would have hurt me worse if I had gone back and divorce was the only option, I don't think I was wrong to leave him. The detectives were convinced that he was dangerous, and I needed to escape. In their opinion, divorce was the only way I was going to continue breathing.

I struggle with other people's opinions that I married him "in sickness and in health." They ask, "Doesn't that count as a mental illness?" Perhaps not in those specific words, but the "what did you do?" rings in their questions.

While Josh and I were talking about my writing this book and sharing our story, he made an insightful remark. Although neither of us would have chosen the path that brought us together, we would not be the same without those past experiences.

Josh divulged that he had planned to propose to his girlfriend the day she told him she had found someone else and had broken up with him. His deep hurt took years to heal. But without that happening, he wouldn't have been ready for love when he met me.

Every relationship has to give and take, as the saying goes, but God made Josh fit me perfectly. For example, Josh is a planner. I tease him that he has plans, backup plans, and his backup plans have backup plans. I can see that God uses Josh's planning to calm my anxiety, and I can trust him.

On the other hand, I, too, like to plan, but I inspire Josh to be more lighthearted and to have fun, allowing him to relax in ways he didn't before we were married. Our family fun includes green mashed potatoes on St. Patrick's Day, drawing on the sidewalk with colored chalk and running through the sprinkler on a hot summer day. We are on the same page on all of the big stuff in life, from our sex life to our finances to parenting. I still have to pinch myself sometimes to prove that this good life is real and that it's mine. God has given me a happily ever after.

32. FINAL THOUGHTS

"For thou hast delivered my soul from death: wilt not thou deliver my feet from falling, that I may walk before God in the light of the living?" – Psalm 56:13 KJV

As I discovered that I was in an abusive situation, I found strength in trusting God and my sincere friends. These women and men encouraged me to get help and stayed with me, despite the personal danger, to make sure I was safe. I learned to trust God when I wondered where I was going to live, or even IF I were going to live.

My situation was horrendous. Unfortunately, it is not uncommon. Domestic violence is an all-too-frequent evil that transcends stereotypes of socio-economic, ethnic, and educational levels. As a survivor, I can share that my abuse became a twisted-normal. I was conditioned and bullied into believing that this violent relationship was just how all marriages were. I could not comprehend anything different at the time.

The Christian circles, in which I lived my entire life were unprepared to help me. We were never allowed to discuss domestic violence or even divorce in the churches I attended, except to say that God hates divorce. When I dared to reach out to pastors and Christian friends, I found no help, and worse; I ended up with more bruises.

When I found myself with no other option except divorce, I was condemned. I know now that those teachings are wrong. God does hate divorce, but He also hates to see wedding vows broken, and above all else, He hates to see His children abused and abandoned. There are worse things than divorce.

I know; I lived them.

God promises, "Behold; I will do a new thing; now it shall spring forth; shall ye not know it? I will even make a way in the wilderness and rivers in the desert" (Isaiah 43:19 KJV). He has! God has blessed me with a new life, different and happy.

Ally is now a teenager. She knows that she and I are still in danger. Every so often, Dirk contacts me to say he will sign off his parental rights because he needs the money that Ally and I get as child support. It has become a routine where we forward his email to our lawyer. Our lawyer writes him a letter, and Dirk sends back a diatribe about how bad a mother I am, and someday he's going to find Ally to tell her how I betrayed him and ruined his life.

We don't respond, except to be disappointed once again that it seems Dirk is still using Ally to upset me. Her counselor suggested that we go to court to remove Dirk's visitation since it was so upsetting to Ally. Thankfully, her counselor wrote a letter to the judge, which, along with our lawyer's arguments, persuaded the judge that Dirk, who represented himself once again, was a danger to Ally. In open court, he exposed his plan to kidnap Ally, taking her to a Caribbean island with no extradition treaty with the United States. The judge decided Dirk should not be allowed any visitation at all, not even supervised. I was excited to learn that for him to see Ally again, he had to prove not only that he is in counseling for his anger issues, but that he would be "beneficial" to Ally's life. The family court law requires him to prove that he would be somehow good for her. I don't think it will ever happen, but only God knows.

We are cautious, keeping our address and personal information private. We alerted Ally's high school, giving them a picture of him and reminding them to check the identification of anyone who comes to pick her up. The local police have an alert on our address, and our home has a security system.

God has blessed us in the past, and we can continue to trust Him to keep us safe, despite these threats. One of my favorite Psalms begins, "He that dwelleth in the secret place of the Most High shall abide under the shadow of the Almighty. I will say of the Lord; He is my refuge and my fortress; my God; in Him will I trust." (Psalm 91:1-2 KJV).

My faith has drastically changed since the day my face hit the glass of our storm door in Washington. Instead of a religion where I contentedly followed the rules set by the church, I now have a relationship with my Heavenly Father based on love, trust, and gratitude for all He has done for me. My connection isn't with a church; it's with God.

My confidence in my Heavenly Father has grown immensely. I am learning that my works show my faith and that those works, including the lists of do's and don'ts I used to believe in so fervently, aren't enough by themselves. "Suppose a brother or a sister is without clothes and daily food. If one of you says to them, 'Go in peace; keep warm and well fed,' but does nothing about their physical needs, what good is it? In the same way, faith by itself, if it is not accompanied by action, is dead." (James 2:15-17 NIV).

Through all the hardship, I gained the knowledge that, although God gives rules for us to keep us from sin, what He desires most is a personal connection with each and every one of us. "And without faith, it is impossible to please God: because anyone who comes to him must believe that he exists and that he rewards those who earnestly seek him." (Hebrews 11:6 NIV).

God miraculously continues to bless me, despite my scars, and sometimes I think because of them. God has never left me alone, even in my darkest hours. From the point where Dirk could have killed me by throwing me down the stairs to living in hiding at Chloe's and Alice's homes, to meeting Josh, getting married, and living an amazing new life as a family, God sent me help and hope and has always taken care of us. God worked behind the scenes to keep me safe, and that experience helps me trust that He will take care of us in the future.

"For I know the thoughts that I think toward you, saith the

Lord, thoughts of peace, and not of evil, to give you an expected end" (Jeremiah 29:11 KJV).

No matter what you are going through, God will take care of you, too.

ABOUT KHARIS PUBLISHING

Kharis Publishing is an independent, traditional publishing house with a core mission to publish impactful books, and channel proceeds into establishing mini-libraries or resource centers for orphanages in developing countries, so these kids will learn to read, dream, and grow. Every time you purchase a book from Kharis Publishing or partner as an author, you are helping give these kids an amazing opportunity to read, dream, and grow. Kharis Publishing is an imprint of Kharis Media LLC. Learn more at https://www.kharispublishing.com

Made in the USA
Monee, IL
15 January 2021